6480

AMERICA the BEAUTIFUL

ARKANSAS

By Ann Heinrichs

Consultants

C. Fred Williams, Ph.D., Professor of History, University of Arkansas at Little Rock

Nadyne W. Aikman, Social Studies Teacher, Moody Elementary School, White Hall, Arkansas

Robert L. Hillerich, Ph.D., Bowling Green State University

CHILDRENS PRESS®
CHICAGO

War Eagle Creek in the Ozarks

Project Editor: Joan Downing
Associate Editor: Shari Joffe
Design Director: Margrit Fiddle
Typesetting: Graphic Connections, Inc.
Engraving: Liberty Photoengraving

Library of Congress Cataloging-in-Publication Data

Heinrichs, Ann.
  America the beautiful. Arkansas / by Ann
Heinrichs.
       p.   cm.
  Includes index.
  Summary: Introduces the geography, history,
government, economy, industry, culture, historic
sites, and famous people of the state known as the
"Land of Opportunity."
  ISBN 0-516-00450-6
  1. Arkansas—Juvenile literature.
[1. Arkansas.] I. Title.
F411.3.H45 1989   88-38529
976.7—dc19   CIP
                                                 AC

A toad-jumping contest during Conway's annual Toad Suck Daze festival

TABLE OF CONTENTS

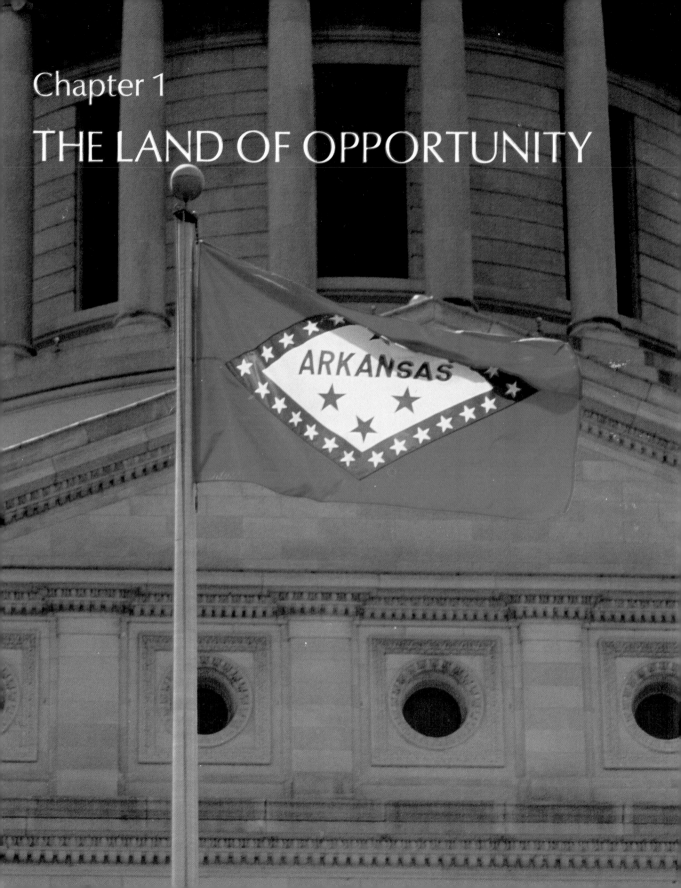

Chapter 1

THE LAND OF OPPORTUNITY

THE LAND OF OPPORTUNITY

"Some of the noblest men and women of America were born and reared in this . . . favored land," wrote novelist Opie Read in 1930. During his years as an Arkansas newspaperman, Read saw firsthand what a tough and imaginative breed Arkansans were.

Back in the 1800s, when Arkansas was nicknamed the Bear State, fierce hunters stalked the Ozark hills for black bears. Traveling through the region and encountering such frontiersmen, Davy Crockett and Jim Bowie felt right at home.

In the 1920s, with frontier days well behind them, Arkansans opened their eyes to the wonders that lay at their feet. Here were vast acres of timberland and valuable minerals and fuels. Here also was a state full of adventurous citizens ready for progress. Lapel buttons reading "I Am Proud of Arkansas" were worn throughout the state. Swept up in the excitement of their new image, state legislators declared Arkansas the Wonder State.

Flood, drought, and depression later took their toll on the state's population and economy. But the optimism of Arkansas's people rose to the fore once again. Aggressive development programs were launched, and in 1953, the state's official nickname became Land of Opportunity.

Hardworking, tough, and as spirited as ever, Arkansans today are moving ahead to forge tomorrow's frontiers.

Chapter 2

THE LAND

THE LAND

"Who can be insensible to the beauty of the verdant hill and valley, to the sublimity of the clouded mountain?" marveled British naturalist Thomas Nuttall as he traveled through Arkansas in 1819. Though the language may sound dated, Arkansas's geographical beauty is ageless.

GEOGRAPHY AND TOPOGRAPHY

Located in the south-central United States, Arkansas is sandwiched between Missouri to the north and Louisiana to the south. The great Mississippi River forms nearly the entire eastern border of the state. Across the river to the east lie the states of Tennessee and Mississippi. Oklahoma extends along most of Arkansas's western edge, while the far southwestern corner borders Texas.

Arkansas's land area covers 53,187 square miles (137,754 square kilometers). In size, it ranks twenty-seventh among the states. Except for Hawaii, Arkansas is the smallest state west of the Mississippi River.

A line drawn across the state from northeast to southwest would show the division between Arkansas's two geographic regions: the highlands and lowlands. The highlands, in the north and west, include the Ozark Plateau, the Ouachita Mountains, and, between them, the fertile Arkansas River Valley. The lowlands in the east and south consist of the Mississippi Alluvial Plain and the West Gulf Coastal Plain.

Mount Nebo State Park lies in the lush Arkansas River Valley.

HIGHLANDS

Extending southward from Missouri, the Ozark Plateau is a region of high tablelands, rugged hills, and deep valleys cut by rushing streams. Along the southern edge of the plateau are the steep gorges of the Boston Mountains. Though much of the Ozark Plateau is wooded, it also contains many small farms.

South of the Boston Mountains lies the Arkansas River Valley. Though it is lower in elevation than the mountain regions to the

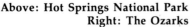

Above: Hot Springs National Park
Right: The Ozarks

north and south, the Arkansas Valley features some of the highest
peaks in the state. Among them is Magazine Mountain, the
highest point in the state, rising sharply to 2,753 feet (839 meters).
Rich coal and natural-gas deposits are found in the western part
of the valley.

South of the Arkansas Valley are the Ouachita Mountains.
These heavily wooded east-west ridges extend into Oklahoma.
The Ouachitas are sparsely populated and just as sparsely farmed.
They provide valuable minerals, as well as timber for construction
and furniture making. The famed hot mineral springs of Hot
Springs National Park are located in the Ouachitas.

The Delta region contains some of the state's best farmland.

LOWLANDS

The eastern one-third of Arkansas, often called the Delta region, is part of the Mississippi Alluvial Plain. The Mississippi Alluvial Plain reaches northward from Louisiana and includes the delta land along the Mississippi River, the Saint Francis River and White River valleys, the Grand Prairie between the Arkansas and White rivers, and a long ridge of hills, called Crowley's Ridge, that runs up to the Missouri border. Once a vast swampland, the Delta region now has some of the best farmland in the state and produces much of the nation's rice.

Southwestern Arkansas is part of the West Gulf Coastal Plain, which extends into Louisiana and Texas. This lowland region has a slightly higher elevation than the eastern alluvial plain. But its pine and white-oak forests are what most distinguish it from the region to the east. Besides timber, the area produces petroleum and natural gas. Farmers raise poultry and livestock in this region.

RIVERS, LAKES, AND SPRINGS

As the Mississippi River flows along the state's eastern border, it leaves behind rich soil deposits. One of the major tributaries of

The White River (left, above) runs through
northern and eastern Arkansas.

the Mississippi River is the Arkansas River. Rising in Colorado's
Rocky Mountains, the Arkansas flows through Colorado, Kansas,
Oklahoma, and across Arkansas on its way to the Mississippi
River.

Once plagued by floods and eroding banks, the Arkansas is now
a major commercial waterway. In 1946, Arkansas Senator John
McClellan and Oklahoma Senator Robert Kerr sponsored a
massive project to stabilize the Arkansas River and make it
suitable for navigation by large commercial vessels. This system of
seventeen locks and dams, called the McClellan-Kerr Arkansas
River Navigation System, was completed in 1970 and opened in
1971. The navigation project allows Pine Bluff, Little Rock, and
Fort Smith access to the Gulf of Mexico.

Arkansas's other major rivers are the White and Saint Francis
rivers in the east, the Ouachita River in the south, and the Red
River in the far southwest.

Almost all of Arkansas's lakes were created as flood-control
reservoirs by damming rivers. Some of the largest are Greers

Ferry, Norfork, Bull Shoals, Beaver, Ouachita, Greeson, DeGray, Millwood, and Felsenthal lakes. Lake Chicot, in southeastern Arkansas, is the state's largest naturally occurring lake. It is an "oxbow" lake, formed long ago as the Mississippi River changed its course.

Many people visit Arkansas for its freshwater springs, whose soothing waters are believed to help relieve some illnesses. The forty-seven springs in the resort town of Hot Springs yield about 1 million gallons (3.8 million liters) of hot water a day. Eureka Springs, high in the Ozarks, has more than sixty springs. Mammoth Spring yields about 235 million gallons (890 million liters) of water per day.

CLIMATE

Arkansas poet John Gould Fletcher knew his state's climate well. "The true Arkansawyer," he wrote, "from June to September, moves slowly, if he moves at all."

Arkansas's summers are indeed hot and humid, and its winters are mild. Temperatures are generally lower and winter snowfalls are heavier in the northern mountains than in the lowlands of the south and east. Yet even in the mountains, winter snowfall seldom exceeds six inches (fifteen centimeters).

Little Rock, in the center of the state, has an average July temperature of 81 degrees Fahrenheit (27 degrees Celsius). In January, Little Rock averages 39.5 degrees Fahrenheit (4 degrees Celsius). The state's highest recorded temperature, a sweltering 120 degrees Fahrenheit (49 degrees Celsius), occurred on August 10, 1936 in the town of Ozark. The state's lowest temperature, minus 29 degrees Fahrenheit (minus 34 degrees Celsius), was recorded in the town of Pond on February 13, 1905.

Arkansas boasts a wide variety
of plants and animals, including
(clockwise from top left) sumacs,
phloxes, white-tailed deer,
cypresses, opossums, alligators,
and corn snakes.

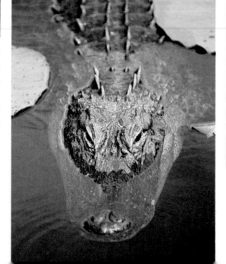

ANIMALS AND PLANTS

Arkansas's forests and lowlands provide many wild animals with shelter and food. Rabbits, squirrels, opossums, raccoons, weasels, woodchucks, skunks, and muskrats live in almost every part of the state. Deer and bears, once rare due to overhunting, are again plentiful. Bobcats and red foxes live in the forests. Armadillos, native to the southwestern United States, have now ventured into Arkansas. Unfortunately, hunting has destroyed the state's populations of wolves, panthers, and buffalos.

Arkansas's lakes and rivers yield trout, bream, crappie, perch, buffalofish, catfish, and several kinds of bass. The state is home to many species of turtles, lizards, and frogs. Alligators can be found in the swamps around the Red River. Most of the snakes in Arkansas, such as king snakes, black snakes, garter snakes, and blue racers, are nonpoisonous. Poisonous species in the state include water moccasins, rattlesnakes, copperheads, and coral snakes.

Songbirds common to Arkansas include cardinals, blue jays, mockingbirds (the state bird), robins, nuthatches, and brown thrashers. Many species of wild ducks and geese feed on the rice fields of the Grand Prairie as they migrate along the Mississippi Flyway.

Half of Arkansas is covered with forest. Loblolly and shortleaf pine are most common in the southern forests. The Ouachita and Ozark forests are made up of mixed pines and hardwoods. Trees common throughout the state include oak, ash, hickory, gum, willow, redbud, dogwood, buckeye, and basswood. Arkansas's wildflowers include black-eyed Susans, passionflowers, water lilies, bellflowers, and orchids. A rare fern, *Woodsia scopulina*, grows on Magazine Mountain.

Chapter 3
THE PEOPLE

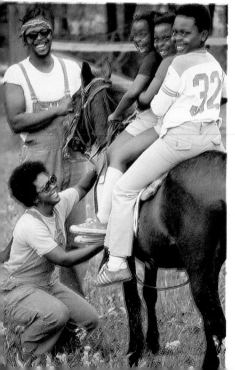

THE PEOPLE

It is difficult to define the typical Arkansan. Novelist Opie Read called Arkansans "some of the noblest men and women of America." Frontiersman Davy Crockett expressed his admiration in a slightly different way. "If I could rest anywhere," he said, "it would be in Arkansaw, where the men are of the real half-horse, half-alligator breed such as grow nowhere else on the face of the universal earth. . . . "

Perhaps the most typical Arkansan trait is a frontier spirit of rugged individualism. When the mayor of Eureka Springs recently described his townspeople, he easily could have been speaking for the whole state. Eureka Springs, he told a reporter, had "more opinions per capita than any other place in the country."

Culturally, the various regions of the state differ more than they resemble each other. Residents of western and central Arkansas tend to align themselves with westerners and midwesterners. Those who live in the south and the east identify more with the Deep South. People of the northern hills share a centuries-old mountaineer spirit with Ozarkers in neighboring Missouri.

POPULATION AND POPULATION DISTRIBUTION

Arkansas ranks thirty-third in the nation in number of residents, with a population of 2,286,419 according to the 1980 census. In 1900, more than 90 percent of Arkansans lived in rural areas; only 10 percent of the population was urban. After 1940, the population shifted slowly from rural to urban areas. By 1960,

Capitol Avenue
in Little Rock

43 percent of Arkansans were urban dwellers. By 1970, the number had increased to 50 percent. Today, more than half the people in the state live in urban areas. Still, there is plenty of space for everyone. Arkansas averages about forty-three people per square mile (seventeen people per square kilometer), while the United States as a whole averages sixty-seven people per square mile (twenty-six people per square kilometer). Little Rock, the state capital, has the largest population, with 158,915 residents. Nearly 394,000 people live in Little Rock's metropolitan area. Fort Smith is the state's second-largest city. Other major Arkansas cities are North Little Rock, Pine Bluff, Fayetteville, and Hot Springs.

Although Arkansas was ruled by Europeans from 1686 to 1803, few whites settled in the region during this time. In 1810, a census

In recent years, many older people have settled in Arkansas.

counted only 1,062 non-Indian residents in the district. It was the American westward expansion that first brought a significant white population to Arkansas. The population of the state grew steadily throughout the 1800s, and passed the one-million mark for the first time in 1890. There continued to be a gradual rise in population in the following decades. In the 1920s and 1930s, however, the population grew more slowly. After Arkansas's population reached 1,949,387 in 1940, the number of residents began to drop as people left the state in search of better jobs. A reversal of this trend began in the 1970s, but it was not until 1980 that the state's population had caught up with—and passed—its 1940 level. The state grew almost 19 percent between 1970 and 1980. Forecasters expect this growth to continue and predict a population of over 2.5 million by 1990. Although many new industries have come to the state, Arkansas's population growth is also due in part to the many retirees who have flocked to the state in recent years.

**Young Arkansans
on a slide at
Pinnacle Mountain
State Park**

ETHNIC MIX

Ninety-nine percent of Arkansans were born in the United
States, and more than 75 percent were born in Arkansas. Many of
the state's people are descended from English, Scottish, and
Scotch-Irish families from the Appalachian region and other
southern states.

An influx of foreign immigrants occurred during the 1800s.
Germans, Italians, and many others made their way to Arkansas
to farm or to work for railroad, mining, and lumbering
companies. A number of ethnic groups, including Chinese and
Lebanese, settled along the Mississippi River in the east.

As a tribute to the lands they left behind, immigrants gave Old World names to many of their towns. Some of the town names to be found on an Arkansas map include Paris, Stuttgart, Prague, Berlin, Hamburg, Antioch, Moscow, Palestine, and Parthenon.

Black people make up more than 16 percent of Arkansas's population. Most black Arkansans are descended from former slaves. Though blacks reside throughout the state, most live in Little Rock and in the eastern and southeastern parts of the state.

POLITICS

For most of its history, Arkansas as a whole has been loyal to the Democratic party. Republican governors served in Arkansas during the Reconstruction period from 1868 to 1874. However, Winthrop Rockefeller, who was elected in 1966, was the first Republican governor to serve since that time.

Traditionally, Arkansans have supported Democratic presidential candidates as well. In 1968, however, they broke a one-hundred-year trend. That year, the state's electoral votes went to George Wallace, the American Independent party candidate. Arkansans supported Republican Richard Nixon for president in 1972, Democrat Jimmy Carter in 1976, Republican Ronald Reagan in 1980 and 1984, and Republican George Bush in 1988. Little by little, the state is moving away from its one-party tradition.

RELIGION

Baptists make up the largest religious group in Arkansas, followed by Methodists. About two-thirds of the state's population belong to one of these two denominations. Other major religious groups in the state are the Churches of Christ, Presbyterians, Roman Catholics, Episcopalians, and the Assemblies of God. A small number of Jews and Christian Scientists also live in Arkansas.

Conservative Christian beliefs have sometimes affected Arkansas's lawmaking processes. In 1929, a state law prohibiting the teaching of the scientific theory of evolution was passed. Christians who interpreted the Bible literally felt that the theory of evolution was antireligious. The United States Supreme Court struck down the law in 1968. A 1930 law required daily reading of the Bible in Arkansas's public schools. The law was repealed in 1980 after it was ruled unconstitutional.

Arkansas drew worldwide attention in 1981, when the state legislature passed what was known as the "balanced-treatment" act. This law required that public-school science classes give equal treatment to both the theory of evolution and the Bible's story of creation. After a celebrated trial, this law, too, was judged unconstitutional.

As early as 1870, religious issues put Arkansas in the international spotlight. That year, Roman Catholic bishops from all over the world convened in Rome, Italy, for a Vatican Council. The council had been called to settle several important issues in the church.

One issue that was brought before the bishops for a vote was the dogma (teaching) of papal infallibility. This doctrine held that the pope—the leader of the Roman Catholic Church—cannot err when making an official declaration of church teachings. Only two bishops in the entire worldwide council cast dissenting votes. One of the two was the Right Reverend Edward Fitzgerald of Little Rock. Even in Rome, the voice of Arkansas individualism could be heard, loud and clear.

Chapter 4

THE BEGINNINGS

THE BEGINNINGS

The word *prehistoric* usually conjures up images of dinosaurs and other gigantic beasts roaming through forests and swamps millions of years ago. Archaeological evidence indicates that dinosaurs did inhabit Arkansas at one time. However, the term *prehistoric* can also refer to more recent times.

Historic times are those that people have described in written records. When the first Europeans arrived in Arkansas in 1541 and wrote of their discoveries, the state's official historic period began. All of the information about Arkansas up to that time is called prehistoric.

PREHISTORIC ARKANSAS

By studying human, animal, and plant remains, archaeologists have pieced together a picture of prehistoric Arkansas. The ancestors of today's American Indians, called Paleo-Indians, lived in Arkansas as early as 10,000 B.C. These people were hunters and gatherers who moved from place to place in search of food. Paleo-Indian weapon points of expertly chipped stone have been found throughout the state.

By 8000 B.C., Arkansas's environment and climate were much as they are today. Around this time, early Arkansans began forming larger social groups. They fashioned many different kinds of stone tools and weapons. For food they relied on plants, nuts, and berries and hunted deer and other game animals. People who

Archaeologists have learned much about prehistoric Arkansans by excavating ancient burial sites (above) and studying such artifacts as this woven basket (right), found preserved in a dry bluff shelter in the Ozark Mountains.

lived along the riverbanks also enjoyed shellfish. Midden heaps (refuse heaps) found along the White, Red, and Ouachita rivers contain empty shells left by these early peoples.

Other people made their homes in the caves and bluffs of northwest Arkansas during this period. Woven cloth, woven grass baskets, and wooden objects have been found in their shelters.

By 1000 B.C., Indians in eastern Arkansas were developing a more stable society. They settled in villages, made pottery, and cultivated crops for food. Like some other Indian groups in North America, they buried their dead in huge, earthen hills. The Indians constructed these burial mounds by piling soil—basketful by basketful—upon the gravesites of their dead. A number of mounds from this period have been discovered in eastern Arkansas along the Mississippi River. Near Helena, archaeologists are studying a group of such burial sites.

Among the many prehistoric artifacts that have been uncovered in Arkansas are these expertly chipped spear points (right), which were found at the Toltec Mounds (above) and date from A.D. 700-950; and this engraved Caddo bottle (left), which dates from 1100-1300.

Indians in the Ozark Mountain region of the state continued to live as they had for centuries. By A.D. 700, however, Indian groups in the southern and eastern lowlands were developing complex ways of life. They grew corn, beans, and squash and hunted small game with bows and arrows. Their many styles of pottery suggest that they traded with, or learned from, other Indians throughout the southeastern United States.

"TOLTEC" MOUNDS

In the mid-1800s, Gilbert Knapp discovered huge mounds on his property southeast of Little Rock. Thinking the mounds had been built by the Toltec Indians of Mexico, he named them the Toltec Mounds. Although archaeologists later found that the Toltecs had not built the mounds, the name remains.

It was the Indians of what is called the Plum Bayou Culture who built these mounds, probably between A.D. 700 and 950. Built in a pattern that suggests a town plaza, the mounds seem to be arranged in relation to the varying positions of the sun. Some are dome-shaped burial mounds; others are flat-topped platforms that may have been used as bases for temples and houses. A pond formed one border of the settlement, and a tall earthen wall enclosed the other sides.

The Plum Bayou people of central Arkansas lived a stable, settled life. They farmed corn, beans, and squash. They also fished and hunted occasionally and lived in sturdy homes. The mound area was a social, religious, and political center for people in the vicinity. Archaeologists believe that religious ceremonies took place in temples on the higher mounds. The lower platforms supported the houses of community leaders.

A mound site in Parkin flourished around the same time. The structures in this settlement, too, are arranged around a central plaza. Fortifications surrounded the village, and platform-topped mounds supported temples and homes. As in the Toltec site, the central village was probably the governing center for people in the surrounding area.

By the 1500s, various American Indian groups had settled in many of the nonmountainous regions of Arkansas. Before 1700, Indian villages were concentrated along the Arkansas and Red rivers in southwestern Arkansas. Northwestern Arkansas was a hunting territory for the Osage Indians. Archaeologists believe that southeastern Arkansas was occupied by groups living in scattered villages.

By 1700, the principal Indian groups in the area included the Quapaws, concentrated around the mouth of the Arkansas River; the Caddos, at the bend of the Red River; and the Osages, who hunted and controlled much of the region north of the Arkansas River.

EUROPEANS ARRIVE

In the spring of 1541, Spanish explorer Hernando De Soto arrived in Arkansas. Weary and half-starved, he and his men were looking for legendary cities of gold. Since 1539, they had wandered through present-day Florida, Georgia, Alabama, and Mississippi. They crossed the Mississippi River on rafts, and are believed to have landed south of Helena at a spot called Sunflower Landing.

The Spaniards continued their travels through Arkansas, encountering many Indian groups but no riches or cities of gold. Historians are not sure of De Soto's exact route. However, it is known that during the harsh winter of 1541, many of the men died of disease or starvation. De Soto himself died of malaria in May 1542, just south of what is now Arkansas's southern border.

It was 132 years before the next Europeans visited Arkansas. In 1673, French explorers Louis Jolliet and Father Jacques Marquette canoed down the Mississippi River to the mouth of the Arkansas River. Friendly Quapaw Indians there warned them to go no farther, so they turned back. Nine years later, another Frenchman, René-Robert Cavelier, Sieur de La Salle, traveled down the Mississippi River to the Gulf of Mexico. He claimed the entire Mississippi River Valley, including the land of present-day Arkansas, for France. He named the territory Louisiana in honor of the French king, Louis XIV.

One of La Salle's officers, Henri de Tonti, returned to Arkansas in 1686. He set up a fur-trading post at a Quapaw village near where the Arkansas and White rivers meet. Known as Arkansas Post, it became the first permanent white settlement in Arkansas. It was also the first permanent settlement in the lower Mississippi River Valley.

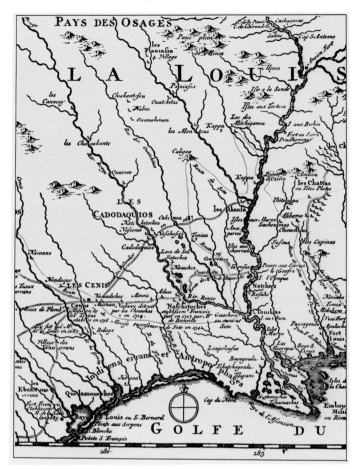

At the time of the first European explorations, the Arkansas region was inhabited by Quapaw Indians (top right).

The earliest Europeans to see Arkansas included De Soto, whose route across the southern United States is traced in the map above; Marquette and Jolliet (bottom left), who canoed down the Mississippi River to the mouth of the Arkansas River in 1673; La Salle (bottom center), who claimed the entire Mississippi Valley for France in 1682; and de Tonti (bottom right), who founded Arkansas Post in 1686.

In the early 1700s, France made several attempts to encourage settlement of the Mississippi Valley. In 1717, the French government permitted a Scottish financier named John Law to implement a huge scheme to bring European settlers to Louisiana. One of the areas he planned to colonize was the area around Arkansas Post. The venture brought several hundred German and Dutch settlers to the area. However, Law's plan ultimately failed, and many of the colonists left the area. About half the settlers stayed and established a colony near Arkansas Post.

THE LITTLE ROCK

Meanwhile, the port of New Orleans was becoming an important trading center. Scouting to establish supply stations and fur-trading posts farther up the Mississippi River, French explorer Bénard de La Harpe set out from New Orleans in 1722. After visiting the meager settlement at Arkansas Post, La Harpe headed up the Arkansas River. Surrounded by flatlands for some 150 miles (241 kilometers) of his journey, he finally spotted a rocky promontory on the south bank of the river.

This moss-grown outcropping had long been an important landmark for Indians and trappers in the Arkansas River Valley. It marked the point where the vast lowland plains to the east broke abruptly into the steep and craggy hills that typify northern Arkansas. La Harpe noted the spot in his journal as simply "the point of rocks." In time, the rock became known by local people as the "Little Rock" to distinguish it from a larger stone bluff, known as the "Big Rock," that lay on the north side of the river a few miles upstream. Eventually, the Little Rock became the site of the town that would become Arkansas's capital and most important city.

An artist's
version of
Arkansas Post
at the time of
its founding
in 1686

ARKANSAS BECOMES AMERICAN

Arkansas changed hands in 1763 when France ceded the territory of Louisiana, including the land that is now Arkansas, to Spain. By a secret treaty in 1800, however, Spain returned Louisiana to France.

At the same time, President Thomas Jefferson wanted the Louisiana territory to belong to the United States. He and many other Americans felt it was necessary for the development of America's western frontier. Acquiring Louisiana would give the United States control of the vast Mississippi River system as well as the valuable port city of New Orleans.

In 1803, Jefferson and French Emperor Napoleon Bonaparte agreed to a giant land sale. For about $15 million, the United States bought the Louisiana territory from France. For less than three cents an acre (about one cent per hectare), the Louisiana Purchase doubled the size of the United States.

Chapter 5

GROWING PAINS

GROWING PAINS

At the time of the Louisiana Purchase, Arkansas had fewer than
one thousand white settlers. Many were hunters and trappers
who traveled the region; a few others farmed the land. Conflicts
sometimes arose when settlers tried to clear the Indians' hunting
grounds. At the same time, many whites married Indian women,
creating a population of mixed ancestry.

Some Indian groups in Arkansas were fighting among
themselves, too. The Osage Indians of the Ozarks had forced the
more peaceful Quapaws to move south of the Arkansas River. The
Caddo Indians, who had occupied southwestern Arkansas for
hundreds of years, were gradually moving south and west into
present-day Louisiana and Texas.

FROM TERRITORY TO STATE

Arkansas was considered part of the Louisiana Territory until
1812, when the southern part of the territory became the state of
Louisiana. The northern section of the Louisiana Territory,
including the Arkansas region, became known as Missouri
Territory. More settlers began moving to the huge new frontier
west of the Mississippi River. Also, the government began
awarding tracts of frontier land in the Arkansas region to veterans
of the War of 1812.

The Louisiana Purchase Historical Monument lies at the spot where American surveyors began mapping the Arkansas region in 1815.

To clarify the property boundaries, President James Monroe sent two surveyors to begin mapping the territory in 1815. Near the present-day town of Marianna, Prospect K. Robbins and Joseph C. Brown marked the initial point in their survey. That point is now the site of the Louisiana Purchase Historical Monument.

The tide of westward-bound settlers soon reached Arkansas. In 1819, seven years after the Missouri Territory was formed, Arkansas had a population of fourteen thousand settlers—enough to become a territory. That year, the land of present-day Arkansas (as well as a section of present-day Oklahoma) officially became Arkansas Territory. Arkansas Post became the territorial capital.

The new territory soon found itself caught in the middle of one of the nation's most serious problems. A power struggle was developing in the United States Congress between those members who supported slavery and those who did not. To preserve their power, proslavery congressmen insisted that any new nonslave states or terrritories be balanced by an equal number of slave states or territories. Because of this requirement, Arkansas

Left: An 1804 drawing of an Osage warrior
Above: A section of a United States-Quapaw treaty showing the Arkansas lands ceded by the Quapaws in 1818

Territory was admitted as a slave territory, even though it had a small number of black slaves compared to other southern states.

Many people thought that westward expansion of the United States was all-important. Competition for land was fierce, and considerable pressure was put on the government to open Indian lands for settlement. Consequently, the federal government began to remove Indian groups from their homelands east of the Mississippi River to make way for white settlers. The Cherokees and Choctaws from the eastern United States were moved into western Arkansas. Arkansas's Quapaw and Osage Indians were moved west to Indian Territory (present-day Oklahoma).

Eventually, the Cherokees and Choctaws were moved to Oklahoma as well.

The arbitrary relocation of Indian peoples aggravated Indian-white relations. Violence often erupted between Indians and whites and even among various Indian groups. In 1817, the government established Fort Smith to keep the peace. The territorial capital was moved from Arkansas Post to Little Rock in 1821. Meanwhile, settlers from the East continued to flood into the new territory. The population tripled in only a few years. By 1835, Arkansas's population had risen to fifty thousand—enough to apply for statehood. On June 15, 1836, Arkansas entered the Union as a slave state.

EARLY STATEHOOD

The year after Arkansas was granted statehood, an economic depression spread throughout the nation. Land values dropped dramatically and Arkansas's two banks collapsed. The Arkansas spirit did not collapse, however. One notable example was the dashing soldier and politician Archibald Yell, who was elected as the state's first congressman in 1837.

A career soldier, Yell had fought under Andrew Jackson during the Seminole War and in the 1815 Battle of New Orleans. As president, Jackson rewarded Yell by appointing him an Arkansas territorial judge. In 1840, Yell became the governor of Arkansas, and in 1844 he entered a hotly contested race for Congress. Rumor has it that, during the campaign, Yell paid the residents of Shawneetown fifty dollars to rename their town Yellville—a name that remains today.

Yell won the election, only to resign his seat in 1846 when the Mexican War broke out. Eager to take up soldiering again, Yell led

Many Arkansans left their homes and journeyed west after gold was discovered in California in 1848.

a regiment of Arkansas cavalry volunteers to Mexico. In the Battle of Buena Vista the following year, the Americans won, but Colonel Archibald Yell lost his life.

New territories acquired from Mexico after the war opened up new western lands for settlers. When gold was discovered in California in 1848, the great Gold Rush began. Hundreds of covered wagons full of gold seekers stopped at Fort Smith and Van Buren to load up on supplies as they followed the westward trail to California. Though these border towns flourished with the supply trade, they also lost many residents who joined the gold seekers.

By the 1850s, the state's economy was thriving. Arkansas mines continued to produce zinc, lead, iron, coal, and other minerals. Lumber mills processed the state's rich supply of timber. From factories and mills came cotton and wool thread, flour, and meal. Steamboats chugged up and down the Arkansas River bringing these goods to market. By 1850, the state's economy was booming once again.

At the same time, cotton plantations were flourishing in the Mississippi Delta region in the southern and eastern part of the state. Planters from other states began to arrive too, and slavery was gaining a foothold in Arkansas. By 1860, Arkansas ranked sixth among the nation's cotton-producing states, and black slaves made up more than one-fourth of the state's population. Still, there were fewer slaves in Arkansas than in any other southern state.

CIVIL WAR

Arkansas's free-spirited growth stopped abruptly in 1861, when the nationwide debate over the issues of slavery and states' rights finally tore the country in two. When Abraham Lincoln was elected president in November 1860, southern slaveholders feared for their plantation economy. Convinced that Lincoln would abolish slavery, seven southern states seceded (withdrew) from the United States. In February 1861, they formed the Confederate States of America, and in April, the Civil War began.

Many Arkansans hesitated to join the Confederacy. Farmers in northern and western Arkansas did not depend on slave labor and preferred to stay within the Union. At a convention in March 1861, Arkansans voted against secession. The state's pro-Union position lasted barely a month, though. When President Lincoln

The 1862 Battle of Pea Ridge was the most important Civil War battle to occur in Arkansas.

called for loyal troops to fight for the Union, Arkansas governor Henry Rector sent his reply: "In answer to your requisition for troops . . . I have to say that none will be furnished." At another convention in May 1861, Arkansas delegates voted to secede from the Union.

Though officially a Confederate state, Arkansas remained divided. About sixty-six thousand Arkansans fought for the Confederacy, but almost fifteen thousand men from northern Arkansas fought for the Union side.

Union and Confederate forces clashed in a number of skirmishes throughout the state. Battles were fought at Poison

Union forces marched into Little Rock in September 1863.

Springs, Marks Mill, Monticello, Arkansas Post, Jenkins Ferry, Helena, Duvalls Bluff, Batesville, and Chalk Bluff. The Battle of Pea Ridge, in March 1862, was the most important Civil War battle to occur in Arkansas. More than twenty-six thousand troops were involved in the three-day battle, which was won by the Union side. Though the Confederates won the important battle of Prairie Grove in December 1862, they later had to surrender their stand.

When Union forces took Little Rock in September 1863, the Confederate state government simply moved to Washington, in southwest Arkansas. Harris Flanagin served as Confederate governor there. Meanwhile, another state government, loyal to the Union, was set up in Little Rock in 1864, with Isaac Murphy as governor. The Confederate capital remained in operation until May 1865, a month after the Civil War ended. For more than a year, Arkansas had two state governments and two governors.

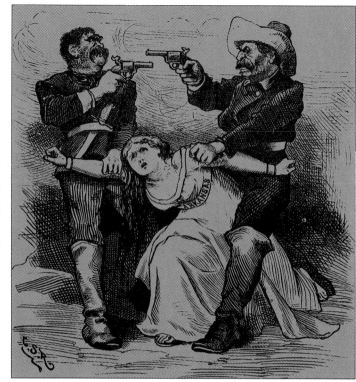

This 1874 cartoon shows Arkansas, represented by a woman, being pulled apart by the warring Brooks and Baxter factions.

RECONSTRUCTION

The Civil War finally ended on April 9, 1865, when Confederate General Robert E. Lee surrendered to Union General Ulysses S. Grant at Appomattox Court House, Virginia. A month later, Arkansas's Confederate governor stepped down.

In a spirit of friendship and forgiveness, President Lincoln planned to immediately readmit the Confederate states to the Union. This process would be known as Reconstruction. But Lincoln was assassinated before he could implement his plans. Without his guidance, Radical Republicans in Congress now saw Reconstruction as a way to punish the South for its rebellion.

With plans to reform southern government and society, northern Republicans known as ''carpetbaggers'' descended on the South. Arkansas, like the other Confederate states, was required to swear loyalty to the Union and to abolish slavery. To enforce Reconstruction, federal troops were stationed in various parts of the state from 1867 to 1874.

In 1868, with Republicans now in control, a new state constitution was drawn up. It gave blacks the right to vote and established free public schools for the first time. A new Republican state legislature also ratified the Fourteenth Amendment to the United States Constitution, which provided citizenship for blacks and gave them full civil rights. Over President Andrew Johnson's veto, Arkansas was readmitted to the Union in June 1868. Republican Powell Clayton then replaced Isaac Murphy as governor.

THE BROOKS-BAXTER WAR

It was not long before the Republican party in Arkansas split into two factions. The regular Republicans were conservatives who aligned themselves with the national Republican party. The liberal Republicans, chafing under the corruption of Republican rule, demanded reform.

In 1872, regular Republican Elisha Baxter ran for governor against liberal Republican Joseph Brooks. Eager to return the state to Democratic rule, the Democrats threw their support to Brooks. Nevertheless, in an election marked by illegal practices on both sides, Baxter won by a narrow margin.

In April 1874, Brooks obtained a court order declaring that he, not Baxter, was the legal governor. At gunpoint, Brooks forced Baxter from his office and took his place. Once again, Arkansas had two men who claimed to be governor.

Before long, supporters of both men took up guns and faced each other along Little Rock's Main Street. President Ulysses S.

The Henderson School in Fayetteville was one of many schools established for blacks by the Freedmen's Bureau during Reconstruction.

Grant sent in federal troops to keep order. Finally, Grant ruled that Elisha Baxter was the legal governor.

GAINS AND LOSSES

Though Reconstruction was a difficult time for Arkansas, the Republicans did bring many lasting reforms to the state. Besides giving civil rights to blacks, they established public schools, founded Arkansas Industrial University (which later became the University of Arkansas), built railroads, and encouraged immigration. They also did their best to control the terrorist racist group known as the Ku Klux Klan.

However, the Brooks-Baxter War was a symptom of the divisions that plagued the Republican party. Though Baxter had been a regular Republican, he eventually won the support of the Democrats by appointing Democrats to important positions. This paved the way for the return of local, Democratic rule in Arkansas. In 1874, Democrat Augustus Garland succeeded Baxter as governor. That same year, a new state constitution was adopted—one that remains in effect today.

During Reconstruction, the federal government took several steps toward insuring civil rights for blacks. In the 1890s, however, most southern states, including Arkansas, found ways of limiting the rights of blacks. Across the South, state legislatures passed "Jim Crow" laws designed to enforce segregation and keep blacks from voting.

HOW DO YOU SAY *ARKANSAS*?

In 1881, the Arkansas state legislature turned its attention to a serious piece of business—how to pronounce the state's name. Since frontier days, the name *Arkansas* had been subjected to various pronunciations. The French, the Spanish, and the Indians each contributed to the confusion.

Legend has it that a Yankee moved to Arkansas, was elected to the legislature, and tried to pass a bill making *Arkansas* rhyme with *Kansas*. To defeat the intruder's bill, a senator named Cassius M. Johnson (who never actually existed) is said to have delivered an impassioned speech on the floor.

"The man who would change the name of Arkansas," Johnson cried, "would . . . hide the stars in a nail-keg, put the sky to soak in a gourd, hang the Arkansas River on a clothes-line, unbuckle the belly-band of time, and turn the sun and moon out to pasture."

Thus, in March 1881, the legislature declared that *Arkansas* should be pronounced "with the final *s* silent . . . and the accent on the first and last syllables." Under no circumstances was the *s* to be sounded or the second syllable accented. In other words, *Arkansas* was to be pronounced "Arkansaw."

Over the years, the speech attributed to this mythical Senator Johnson became more and more outrageous with each retelling. Even Mark Twain tells a version of the story in his *Life on the Mississippi*. Still, the historical fact remains. The legislature did, in fact, establish the official pronunciation in 1881.

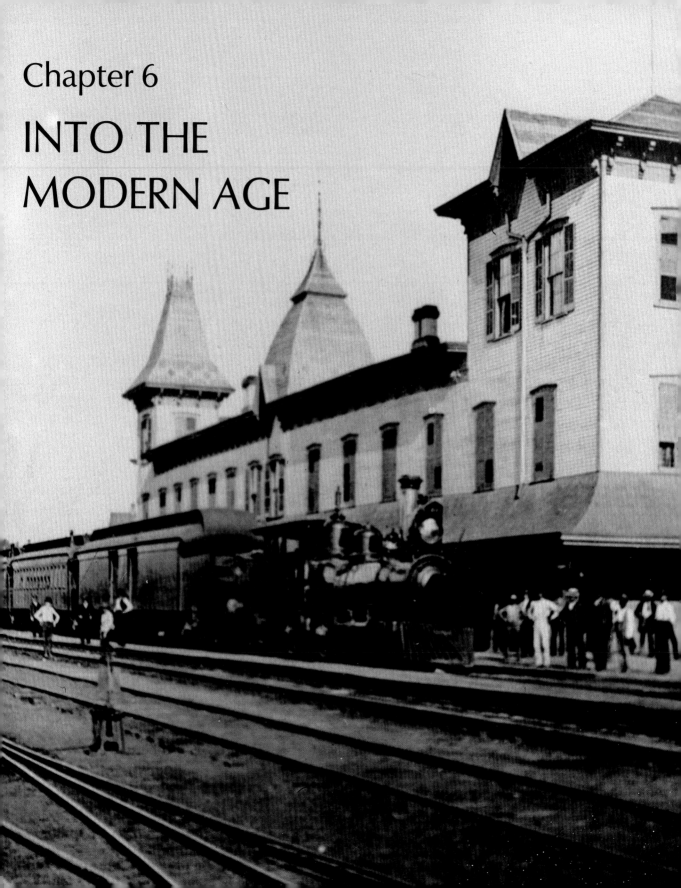

Chapter 6

INTO THE
MODERN AGE

INTO THE MODERN AGE

The Civil War left behind a state war debt of over $13 million and an empty state treasury. To address the problem, Arkansas's political leaders encouraged big business, particularly railroad building. Railroad companies in turn lured American and foreign immigrants to the state to settle along the rail routes. To make more farmland available, swamps were drained and timberland was cleared. Though cotton was still the state's major agricultural product, farmers were beginning to raise more rice and soybeans, as well as fruit, livestock, and poultry. Bauxite, the ore from which aluminum is made, was discovered in 1887 near Little Rock. Coal mining was a growing industry in the south. The new railroads enabled producers of timber, coal, and bauxite to transport their goods easily to processing plants and markets.

THE AGRARIAN REVOLT

Arkansas farmers, however, were not prospering. In the late 1880s, farm prices dropped and a drought swept the state. The farmers felt that the railroads' profits were being made at the farmers' expense. Arkansas's Democratic leaders were of no help, for they continued to favor big business.

In what became known as the Agrarian Revolt, Arkansas farmers banded together and formed a political party called the Agricultural Wheel. Known as the Wheelers, these farmers numbered almost five thousand members by 1884. Sharing a militant sense of brotherhood, they rallied to the strains of their rousing "Wheel Poem":

> Come all ye sunburnt sons of toil,
> Arise from thine oppression;
> 'Tis true we till the stubborn soil,
> But a highway to progression,
> Which enemies cannot conceal,
> Is opened by this mighty Wheel.
>
> Come, let us join our hearts and hands,
> And set this Wheel a-going;
> Perhaps 'twill roll to other lands,
> Its seeds of fortune sowing,
> 'Till all the world its power may feel,
> And bless the Agriculture Wheel.
>
> Heed not the idle words of those
> Who would our march to freedom stay.
> They get their money, food and clothes
> From us who labor day by day;
> And if they could, I guess they'd steal
> The power and glory of the Wheel.

The Wheelers' sense of solidarity extended beyond state lines. These disgruntled farmers allied themselves with national labor unions that opposed monopolies, railroads, and the financial kings of the East. Nationwide, dissatisfaction among farmers led to the formation of the Populist, or People's, party. In Arkansas, the Democratic party needed a strong leader to lure back the dissident farmers. The time was ripe for a Democratic champion of the "common man"—and that champion was Jeff Davis.

JEFF DAVIS

Named after Confederate president Jefferson Davis, Jeff Davis hit the campaign trail for governor in 1900 with speeches as

Jeff Davis was governor of Arkansas from 1901 to 1907.

colorful as his flaming red hair. Attacking big meat businesses and their high prices, he declared, " . . . the prices of meat are so high that I can hardly buy breakfast bacon. . . . I just buy one slice, hang it up by a long string, and let each one of my kids jump up and grease their mouths. . . . " Lashing out at Arkansas newspapers that sided with big-money interests, Davis said, " . . . if I find [my little boy] has not a bit of sense upon earth, I am going to make an editor out of him and send him to Little Rock to edit the *Arkansas Democrat.* . . . " Spying some copies of the *Arkansas Gazette* in the audience during a speech, Davis said, "I had rather be caught with a dead buzzard under my arm, or a dead polecat."

Davis was elected governor in 1900 and served three terms. During that time, he stopped wasteful state spending, regulated businesses more fairly, reformed prisons and state government, sponsored new labor laws, and paid off much of the state's debt.

After Davis left office in 1907, the governorship reverted to the conservative Democrats. Even so, Arkansans continued to enjoy steady social and economic progress. Governor George Donaghey,

The worst flood in Arkansas history occurred when the Mississippi and Arkansas rivers overflowed in 1927.

who served from 1909 to 1913, created a state board of education and a state board of health. Charles Brough, a former University of Arkansas professor who served as governor from 1917 to 1921, brought great improvements in education during his term. And, it was during Brough's term that Arkansas granted women the right to vote—becoming the first southern state to do so.

ECONOMIC PROBLEMS AND SOLUTIONS

The year 1920 brought the first of many economic ups and downs for the state. That year, a sharp drop in cotton prices severely hurt Arkansas farmers. Although rice and soybean farming were on the rise, the state's farmers were still largely dependent on cotton. In 1927, the Arkansas and Mississippi rivers flooded, leaving one-fifth of the state temporarily covered by water. The flood laid waste to millions of acres in the Delta region. The nation's entire plains region was devastated by a severe

Arkansas migrants in California during the Great Depression of the 1930s

drought that began in 1930, and the Great Depression brought massive unemployment and even lower farm prices. Because of road-building debts, the state treasury was almost bankrupt by 1933.

These difficulties brought renewed interest in improved farming methods. Conservation programs were initiated to guard against future land loss from drought. Federal public-works projects helped the state recover from the depression. Many buildings, including schools, post offices, and other public buildings, were built with federal aid.

BUDDING PROSPERITY

Arkansas's economic decline began to reverse during World War II. With the aid of wartime industries, the state's economy gradually shifted from agricultural to industrial. The state's aluminum industry flourished with increased mining of bauxite. Oil and natural gas had been discovered in El Dorado in 1921 and Smackover in 1922. The great wartime demand for these fuels boosted Arkansas's petroleum industry.

Arkansas-born General Douglas MacArthur served as commander of the Allied forces in the Pacific during World War II.

After the United States entered the war in 1941, more than two hundred thousand Arkansans joined the fighting forces. Arkansans were especially proud of one native son: General Douglas MacArthur, commander of the Allied forces in the Pacific.

Many changes were occurring on Arkansas's farms. Farm machinery was doing work that had formerly been carried out by farm workers. Although the state's industries were expanding, they could not grow fast enough to provide jobs for all the unskilled farm workers. As a result, many Arkansans left the state to find work elsewhere. The state legislature had no choice but to make an all-out effort to recruit new industries to the state. In 1953, it changed the state's official nickname from the Wonder State to Land of Opportunity. Then, in 1955, the legislature created the Arkansas Industrial Development Commission (AIDC). The commission was charged with attracting industry to

Elizabeth Eckford (above) was one of nine black students who enrolled at Little Rock's all-white Central High School in 1957. On September 25, the students were escorted into the school by federal troops that had been called in to enforce the desegregation ruling (right).

the state. By the early 1960s, Arkansas's manufacturing income finally surpassed its farm income. By 1970, the state's population had almost reached its 1940 level.

THE LITTLE ROCK SCHOOL CRISIS

In the midst of its industrial rebirth, Arkansas still lagged behind much of the rest of the country in the area of civil rights. The United States Supreme Court had ruled in 1954 that having separate public schools for white and black students was unconstitutional. In 1957, nine black students enrolled in Little Rock's all-white Central High School.

On the first day of school, Governor Orval Faubus called out Arkansas National Guard troops to block the black students from entering the school. The incident drew national attention, and tensions ran high. President Dwight D. Eisenhower ordered federal troops to enforce the integration ruling.

At the start of the 1958-59 school year, the state legislature allowed Faubus to close Little Rock's public high schools. If the schools were closed, Faubus reasoned, they could not be integrated. Finally, in 1959, Little Rock's schools reopened—to both blacks and whites. Gradually, the rest of the state began to integrate its public schools and other public facilities.

Governor Faubus served six consecutive terms, the longest tenure of any Arkansas governor. However, the school crisis and a state prison scandal in the 1960s plagued his later years in office.

A REPUBLICAN VICTORY

In 1967, Arkansans welcomed their first Republican governor since Reconstruction days—wealthy cattleman Winthrop Rockefeller. A New Yorker who had moved to Arkansas in 1953, Rockefeller had been chairman of the Arkansas Industrial Development Commission. Its success was attributed to his leadership. As governor, Rockefeller introduced many reforms in the state government.

Democrats regained the governorship in 1970. An energetic young Democrat named Dale Bumpers, who later became a United States senator, defeated Rockefeller after beating Faubus in the Democratic primary. But the Republican party in Arkansas had come back to life. In 1972, Republican presidential candidate Richard Nixon became the first Republican to win the state's electoral vote since 1868.

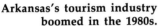
Arkansas's tourism industry
boomed in the 1980s.

LOOKING TO THE FUTURE

In the 1980s, Arkansas continued its economic growth. The state's population and per-capita income both continued to rise. The drive to bring new business to the state also continued. Nationwide promotion helped the new industries of recreation and tourism to thrive. Drawn to Arkansas's unspoiled natural beauty, older people from all over the country are spending their retirement years in the state.

Still, many challenges remain in the Land of Opportunity. Counties in the Delta region are extremely poor, and the farm economy is struggling. But state officials are optimistic. With the typical Arkansan spirit of progress, Arkansans are working to improve the public-school system, combat poverty and unemployment, and increase public services. As the twenty-first century nears, Arkansans look forward to seeing their state truly become a land of opportunity for all.

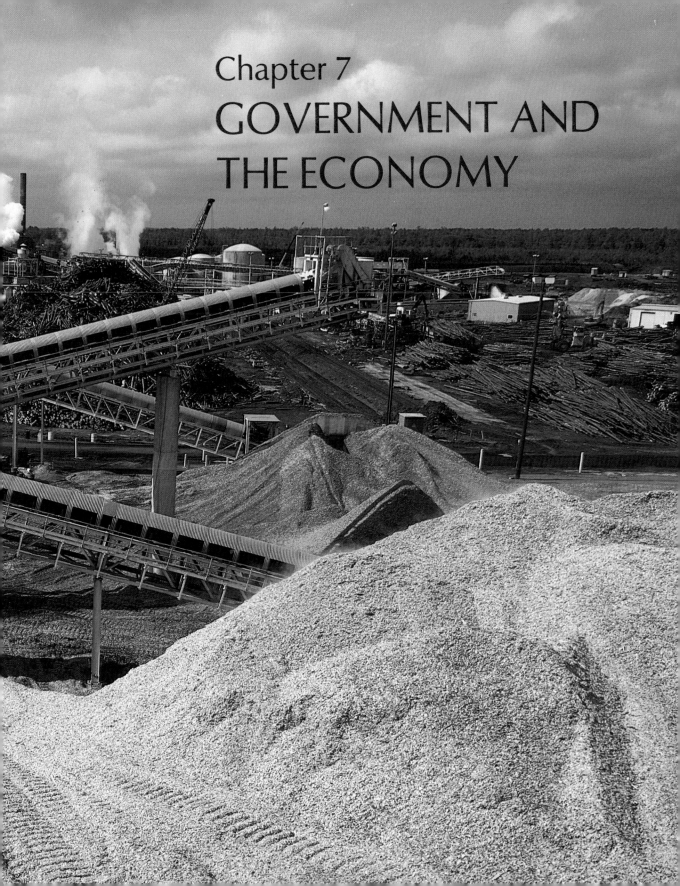

Chapter 7
GOVERNMENT AND THE ECONOMY

GOVERNMENT AND THE ECONOMY

Arkansas has had five state constitutions since it entered the Union in 1836. The present constitution has been in effect since 1874. Amendments, or changes, to the constitution may be made by the state legislature, by voters' petitions, or during a state constitutional convention. In 1980, Arkansas voters rejected a proposal to replace the 1874 state constitution with a new one.

STATE GOVERNMENT

Like most other states, Arkansas patterns its state government after the federal government. The governing power is balanced among three ruling branches: the legislative, which makes the laws; the executive, which carries out the laws; and the judicial, which interprets the laws.

The state legislature, or General Assembly, is Arkansas's chief lawmaking body. Like the United States Congress, it consists of two houses: a senate and a house of representatives. Arkansas's thirty-five senators and one hundred representatives begin regular lawmaking sessions on the second Monday in January of odd-numbered years. Sessions generally last sixty days, and the governor may call special sessions. State senators are elected to four-year terms and state representatives serve two-year terms.

The head of the executive branch is the governor. Other major officials in the executive branch are the lieutenant governor,

The state capitol in Little Rock

secretary of state, attorney general, auditor, treasurer, and land commissioner. The governor and these officers are elected to four-year terms and may be reelected an unlimited number of times. The governor appoints other major state officers.

At the top of the judicial system is the state supreme court. It consists of a chief justice and six associate justices, all elected to eight-year terms. These judges hear appeals, or disputed decisions, from lower courts. Next in order are the circuit courts, which try civil and criminal cases; and the chancery courts, which handle "equity" matters, such as mortgages and domestic relations. In addition, there are county judges, municipal judges, and justices of the peace.

In each of Arkansas's seventy-five counties, a county judge presides over county business. Other county officials are the sheriff, tax collector, assessor, treasurer, county clerk, and coroner. Some cities, including Little Rock, are governed by a city council headed by a manager. Most cities, however, elect a mayor who shares power with the city council.

Government-sponsored projects in Arkansas have included building this dam on the White River.

ARKANSANS IN CONGRESS

Three Arkansans held powerful positions in the United States Congress in the second half of the twentieth century. Senator J. William Fulbright served as chairman of the Senate Foreign Relations Committee from 1959 to 1974 and was outspoken in his opposition to the Vietnam War. He sponsored bills to create the United Nations and the Fulbright Act, which established the distinguished Fulbright Scholarships.

Congressman Wilbur Mills served thirty-eight years in the House of Representatives. As chairman of the House Ways and Means Committee from 1958 to 1975, he influenced nearly all the legislation that passed through the House of Representatives, especially financial and taxation bills.

Senator John McClellan investigated organized crime and labor unions as chairman of the Senate's Permanent Investigations Subcommittee. Later, as chairman of the Senate Appropriations Committee, he kept a watch on federal spending.

McClellan also obtained federal funding for one of Arkansas's largest development projects. Working with Oklahoma senator Robert Kerr, he sponsored the McClellan-Kerr Arkansas River Navigation System project. This massive project opened the Arkansas River for navigation by seagoing vessels. Riverbanks were stabilized, river channels were deepened, and locks and dams were built. The system, which opened in 1971, has boosted Arkansas's mining and manufacturing industries by providing transportation for both finished products and raw materials needed for manufacturing.

STATE INCOME AND SPENDING

Arkansas's state government receives revenue, or income, from three main sources. About one-third of the state revenue comes from sales taxes and taxes on motor fuels, tobacco, alcoholic beverages, and horse racing. Grants from the federal government provide another large source of revenue. Other sources include income taxes from individuals and businesses, and fees for hunting, fishing, and vehicle licenses.

The largest single state expenditure is for public education. Highway construction and public welfare are the next-largest budget items. On the average, Arkansas spends less on education and highways per state resident than do most other states. However, compared to the average income of its residents, Arkansas's expenditures are higher than the national average. In recent years, the percent increase in funds spent on public education has been one of the highest in the nation.

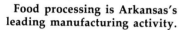
Food processing is Arkansas's leading manufacturing activity.

BUSINESS AND INDUSTRY

Manufacturing is Arkansas's major economic activity, accounting for 26 percent of the gross state product (the annual total value of goods and services produced). Nearly one-fourth of the state's work force is employed in manufacturing. Although manufacturing has surpassed agriculture as a source of income for the state, farming is still a cornerstone of the economy.

Food products account for most of the state's manufactured products. Arkansas's Tyson Foods and Riceland Foods are among the country's leading food-processing corporations. Large food-processing plants are located in Batesville, Berryville, Dardanelle, De Queen, Fayetteville, Springdale, Russellville, and Stuttgart. Among the food products turned out by Arkansas plants are animal feed, canned vegetables, cottonseed oil, milk, meats, poultry, rice, and soft drinks. Electrical equipment, wood and

Left: Workers on an oil rig
Above: Fishing lures being
manufactured in Fort Smith

aluminum products, chemicals, and aircraft parts are just a few of
the state's other manufactured goods.

Many of the top chemical manufacturers in the country operate
plants in Arkansas. An abundance of water, minerals, and other
natural resources has attracted scores of new industries to the
state in recent years. More new businesses, both American and
foreign, are expected to locate in Arkansas in the future.

Service industries produce more than 60 percent of Arkansas's
gross state product. Wholesale and retail trade is the state's
leading service industry. The Bentonville-based Wal-Mart
Corporation operates stores throughout the South and the
Midwest. Dillard Department Stores is another major retail
company in Arkansas. Other important service industries include
finance, insurance, real estate, community and social services, and
government.

Arkansas's tourism industry is enjoying an all-time high.
Travelers to the state's parks, historic sites, and recreation areas
spend about $2 billion in Arkansas every year.

AGRICULTURE

In many parts of Arkansas, prime-time television ads for weed killers, fertilizers, and pesticides reflect the importance of agriculture in the state. Almost half of Arkansas's total land area is farmland. The products of Arkansas's fifty-three thousand farms account for 4 percent of the gross state product.

Arkansas is the nation's number-one producer of broilers (young chickens). Broilers are the state's leading agricultural product; they produce as much income for the state as all of the state's crops combined. Broilers are raised mainly in the northwestern part of the state. Beef cattle are Arkansas's second most-important livestock product. The hardy Santa Gertrudis breed was introduced into Arkansas from west Texas. Other important livestock products are eggs, dairy products, turkeys, and hogs.

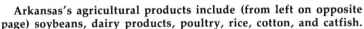
Arkansas's agricultural products include (from left on opposite page) soybeans, dairy products, poultry, rice, cotton, and catfish.

Though cotton was once the state's major cash crop, soybeans now produce the most income for Arkansas farmers. Ironically, soybeans were once used only to return nitrogen to soil that had been worn out by cotton plantings. Arkansas is now the country's eighth-ranked soybean producer.

Rice is the state's second-most-important crop. Arkansas leads the country in rice production, supplying about one-third of the amount grown in the United States. Most of the rice is raised in the Delta region, which has the state's richest farmland. The Grand Prairie, between the Arkansas and White rivers in the Delta region, is an especially important rice-growing area. Early farmers had trouble growing crops on the Grand Prairie because of the hard clay beneath its surface. But it was this same subsoil that made the prairie a natural rice paddy.

Wheat is another major cash crop in Arkansas. Farmers in the state also cultivate sorghum grain, cotton, cottonseed, oats, hay, corn, lespedeza seed, fescue, grapes, snap beans, tomatoes, pecans, and strawberries.

The University
of Arkansas at
Fayetteville

EDUCATION

From its earliest days as a territory, Arkansas has maintained an interest in education. The state's first schools were established by missionaries to teach Indian children. One of the earliest was Dwight Mission, a Cherokee school near Russellville founded in 1820 by Reverend Cephas Washburn. In 1833, in the same county, Albert Pike began teaching classes for the children of white settlers. Pike was paid partly with money and partly with pigs.

In 1819, a section of land in each county of the new Arkansas Territory was set aside for schools. The state legislature called for a public-school system in 1843, though parents who could afford tuition were required to pay. Many chose to send their children to private academies instead. The state constitutions of 1868 and 1874 established a firm public-school system. The Freedmen's Bureau opened the first schools for black students in 1864. After 1909, Arkansas children were required by law to attend school, and after 1937, free textbooks were made available.

Seventy-five percent of Arkansas's students graduate from high school, compared to 71 percent in the nation as a whole. Arkansas high-school students recently ranked twelfth in the nation in Scholastic Aptitude Test (SAT) scores. The combined scores of Arkansas students averaged 999, well above the national average of 893.

Fourteen accredited colleges and universities are scattered throughout the state. The oldest, founded in 1836 by the Presbyterian church, is Arkansas College at Batesville. The University of Arkansas is the state's oldest public university. It opened in 1871 as Arkansas Industrial University and changed its name in 1899.

The University of Arkansas's main campus is in Fayetteville, with branch campuses in Little Rock, Pine Bluff, and Monticello. The University of Arkansas Medical Center at the Little Rock campus trains doctors, nurses, pharmacists, and other medical professionals.

TRANSPORTATION

In its early days, Arkansas's rivers were the state's major transportation routes. Flatboats and keelboats carried people and products down the Arkansas River and its tributaries to the Mississippi River. From there they could travel north to St. Louis or south to the port of New Orleans. Ferries carried people and their cattle, wagons, and other possessions across the rivers. In the early 1800s, steamboats occasionally plied the Arkansas River.

In the second half of the 1800s, railroads gradually replaced river transportation. The railroads linked such Arkansas cities as Little Rock, Pine Bluff, and Camden to each other, as well as to cities outside the state such as Memphis, Tennessee; St. Louis,

Flour for export being loaded onto a barge at Pine Bluff

Missouri; and Tulsa, Oklahoma. The "iron horses" reached their peak in Arkansas in the early 1900s. Since that time, they have gradually declined in importance. Today, four major rail systems run on about 3,600 miles (5,800 kilometers) of track.

River traffic has had its comeback, however, since the opening of the McClellan-Kerr Arkansas River Navigation System in 1971. Now heavy barges can travel through a series of locks and dams from the port of Tulsa, Oklahoma, through Fort Smith, Little Rock, and Pine Bluff to the Mississippi River and beyond.

One of the earliest land trails for Arkansas pioneers was the Grand Prairie Trace, which led from Brinkley to Little Rock alongside present-day Interstate 40. Today Little Rock is the hub of Arkansas's major highways. Interstate 30 leads from there to

Texarkana, continuing on into Texas. Interstate 40 cuts an east-west route across the state. It replaces the legendary Route 66, which stretched all the way from the Atlantic to the Pacific Ocean. West Memphis marks the southern end of Interstate 55, which extends northward to St. Louis and Chicago. In the east, along the Mississippi River, is a network of highways known as the Great River Road. Including its federal and state highways and county roads, Arkansas has a total of about 77,000 miles (124,000 kilometers) of roadways.

Arkansas has eighty-six commercial airports, forty of which can accommodate large business jets. Major passenger and freight airlines service the larger city airports. A network of commuter airlines serves the smaller cities.

COMMUNICATION

The *Arkansas Gazette*, first published at Arkansas Post in 1819, is the oldest continuously published newspaper west of the Mississippi River. Since 1821, it has been published in Little Rock. The *Gazette* and Little Rock's *Arkansas Democrat* are the state's most important newspapers. Other major publications are Fort Smith's *Southwest Times Record* and Texarkana's *Gazette*. About thirty daily and sixty weekly newspapers are published throughout the state.

Little Rock's KATV, Arkansas's first commercial television station, began broadcasting in 1953. Today there are about 15 stations scattered around the state. Arkansas's first radio station, Pine Bluff's WOK, went on the air in 1921. Now Arkansans can tune in to about 150 locally based radio stations. The "Lum and Abner" radio show, which ran every week for twenty-two years, brought nationwide fame to the town of Pine Ridge.

Chapter 8
ARKANSAS FOLKWAYS

ARKANSAS FOLKWAYS

Many of Arkansas's native arts and crafts are based on centuries-old traditions. They were brought by pioneers who migrated in the 1600s from England to Virginia, then to the southern Appalachian region, and finally to Arkansas. Some of the older skills have been lost to modern times. Others have died out and been revived, and a few have survived through centuries of change.

HANDCRAFTS

Quilt making is one of Arkansas's oldest native crafts. A trip through the state's mountain areas and small towns takes a traveler past innumerable roadside stands selling unique and colorful handmade quilts. In some areas, mothers still teach their daughters the time-honored patterns, stitches, and techniques of quilting.

Basket weaving and woodworking skills are still alive today. Craft shops sell white-oak baskets of every size and shape. Other crafted items include splint-bottom chairs and furniture tooled with a foot lathe.

Arkansas broom makers fashion more than a dozen styles of brooms, including kitchen brooms, hearth brooms, pot scrubbers, and "cobweb getters." The handles are made from sturdy tree branches, and some have old men's faces, called tree spirits, carved into them. Some brooms are based on designs from the 1700s and 1800s.

Left: An Arkansas craftsman carving a "tree spirit" into a broom handle
Above: A quilter at the Ozark Folk Center in Mountain View

The Ozark Folk Center in Mountain View is dedicated to preserving Arkansas's traditional arts and crafts. Through its workshops and apprenticeship programs, master craftspeople pass on the arts of pottery, candle making, basketry, doll making, blacksmithing, hand-loom weaving, musical-instrument making, and many others. Visitors can stroll through the crafts village and watch these artisans at work.

The Ozark Foothills Craft Guild, also based in Mountain View, was organized in 1962 to revive and preserve traditional crafts. Its members must maintain high standards of workmanship.

MUSIC

In Arkansas there is a musical style for every taste. Folk music based on very old traditions features instruments such as the Autoharp, mandolin, hammered dulcimer, mountain dulcimer, and Dobro.

A serious revival of Arkansas's folk-music tradition began in Stone County in 1963. One of the revivalists was guitarist and folk

The revival of Arkansas folk music that was sparked by such musicians as Jimmy Driftwood (above) led to the creation of the Ozark Folk Center, which hosts the annual Arkansas Folk Festival (right).

singer Jimmy Driftwood, famous for his rousing ballad "The Battle of New Orleans." Driftwood and other local musicians banded together and called themselves the Rackensack Folklore Society. Every Friday night, the Rackensacks brought their various instruments down to the county courthouse and played and sang, sometimes until dawn. Soon the Rackensacks were drawing audiences by the thousands. The enthusiasm they sparked eventually led to the creation of the Ozark Folk Center. The folk center now holds workshops and contests for players of many traditional Ozark instruments. Nightly concerts at the center feature authentic Ozark folk music at its best.

In Eureka Springs, crowds flock to the country-music shows at the Ozark Mountain Hoe-Down and the Pine Mountain Jamboree. Many small towns have their own jamborees, too; some feature "kitchen bands," whose members play rousing tunes on pots and pans, washboards, wash tubs, and other kitchen items.

The eastern and southern part of the state is blues territory. Like their neighbors farther south along the Mississippi River, southeastern Arkansans are drawn to Mississippi Delta-style blues. Texas-style blues can be heard in towns in the southwest.

Bluegrass, country-western, country rock, and folk-rock music all have large followings. Some of the finest fiddling and banjo picking in the world can be heard in Arkansas. And no fiddler's repertoire is complete without the standard fiddle tune "The Arkansas Traveler."

A weekly radio show called "The Folk Sampler" brings traditional Arkansas music to public-radio-station audiences around the country. Produced in Siloam Springs by Mike Flynn, the show features a sampling of folk, bluegrass, blues, and country music.

FOOD

Delicacies of the Deep South and the Southwest, as well as local specialties, may find their way to an Arkansas dinner table. Deep-fried catfish, hush puppies (deep-fried cornmeal balls), and coleslaw make a well-rounded Arkansas meal. Okra, a fuzzy green pod, is delicious either fried in butter or boiled in gumbo, a thick vegetable soup. Black-eyed peas, purple-hull peas, turnip greens, and poke salad are popular side dishes.

Dumplings, cornbread, corn fritters, buttermilk biscuits, and garlic-flavored grits may substitute for ordinary bread. Piccalilli, a sharp and zesty relish, can spice up almost anything.

Arkansas smoked hams are sold in roadside shops all over the state, and ham and red-eye gravy is a morning favorite. The pig also provides chitterlings (intestines, pronounced "chitlins"), spareribs, and fatback (salt pork).

Chicken, the state's top agricultural product, is always a popular entree. It is rumored that an obscure state law requires fried chicken to be eaten with the hands. However, it takes a knife and fork to consume chicken-fried steak, a slab of beef battered and cooked fried-chicken style.

Candied yams appeal to diners with a sweet tooth. For dessert, nothing compares to a fruit cobbler or a rich pecan pie.

TALL TALES

Many regions of the United States have unique native legends and storytelling styles. Arkansas, since its frontier days, has been notorious for its "tall tales." Partly an art form and partly sheer mischief, the tall tale thrives among Arkansas's mountain folk. Ozark folklorist Vance Randolph collected and published hundreds of these tales. One of his collections is appropriately titled *We Always Lie to Strangers*.

The traditional Arkansas storyteller may say the mosquitoes were so big last summer that one of them carried off his cow. Another may say his hog was so skinny it had to stand up twice to cast a shadow.

One of Arkansas's most famous storytellers was himself a fictional character. He was a fearless bear hunter, the hero of Thomas Bangs Thorpe's 1841 short story "The Big Bear of Arkansas." For hours, this hunter entertained steamboat passengers, telling how he hunted the biggest bear of all—a bear that "loomed up like a black mist" in the Arkansas hills. The bear's hide was so big, the hunter claimed, that he made a bedspread out of it, with "several feet on each side to tuck up."

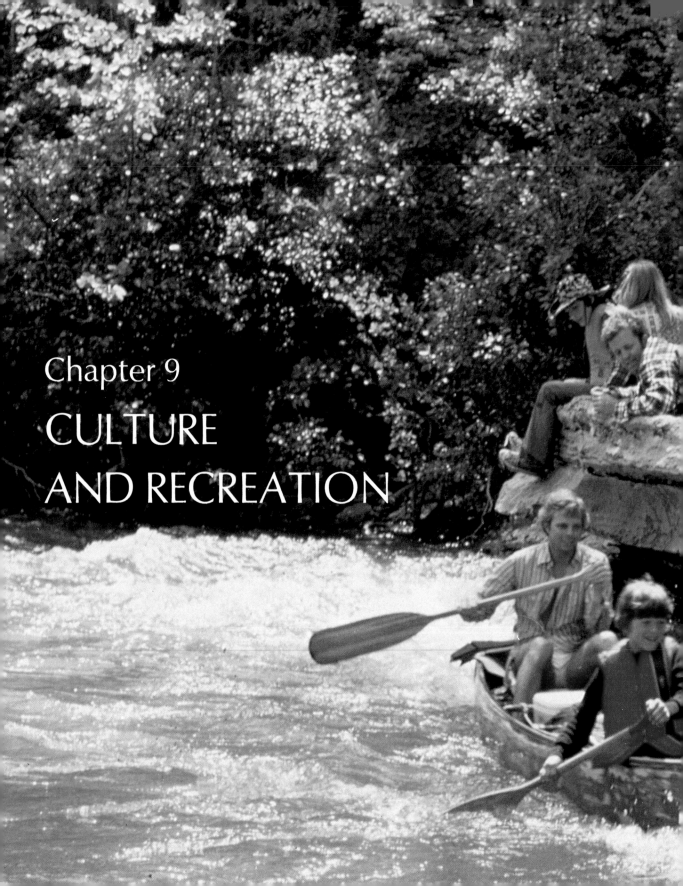

Chapter 9
CULTURE
AND RECREATION

CULTURE AND RECREATION

MUSEUMS

Arkansas's many museums offer fascinating exhibits for visitors interested in history, fine arts, archaeology, and collectors' items. Little Rock's MacArthur Park is home to the Museum of Science and History and the Arkansas Arts Center. The nearby Decorative Arts Museum is housed in the historic Pike-Fletcher-Terry House.

Visitors to Little Rock's Arkansas Territorial Restoration can tour fourteen restored buildings from the state's territorial days. The Old State House, Arkansas's first state capital, houses a state history museum and Granny's Attic, a hands-on collection of historic items.

The University Museum at the University of Arkansas in Fayetteville has historical, archaeological, and mineral exhibits. The Hampson Museum in Wilson features artifacts of Arkansas's Mound Builders. Pine Bluff's Jefferson County Historical Museum includes Quapaw relics. The Southeast Arkansas Arts and Science Center, also in Pine Bluff, presents music, dance, and drama in addition to its art exhibits.

From 1875 to 1896, Judge Isaac Parker, known as the "Hanging Judge" because he sentenced so many outlaws to death, presided over the federal district court at Fort Smith. Called "hell on the border," Parker's courtroom, jail, and gallows are now part of the Fort Smith National Historic Site. The nearby Old Fort Museum displays important artifacts from the area's past.

Left: The Stuttgart
Agricultural Museum
Above: Judge Isaac
Parker's courtroom at
Fort Smith National
Historic Site

Firearms that belonged to Jesse James, Pancho Villa, Billy the Kid, Annie Oakley, and other famous sharpshooters may be viewed at Berryville's Saunders Museum. The Daisy International Air Gun Museum in Rogers contains the largest collection of air rifles in the world.

Calliopes and nickelodeons are among the treats displayed at the Miles Musical Museum in Eureka Springs. The Stuttgart Agricultural Museum in Stuttgart is especially proud of its new waterfowl wing. The Arkansas Oil and Brine Museum in Smackover traces the development of the oil industry in Arkansas. Other fascinating museums include the Josephine Tussaud Wax Museum, Read's Museum of Automobiles, and the Mid-America Museum, all in Hot Springs; the Phillips County Museum in Helena, which features war artifacts; and the Arkansas State University Museum in Jonesboro.

Little Rock is the home of the Arkansas Symphony Orchestra.

PERFORMING ARTS

People in cities and towns throughout the state enjoy performances by local orchestras and drama and choral groups. Little Rock is proud of its Arkansas Symphony Orchestra, Arkansas Repertory Theatre, Arkansas Opera Theatre, Arkansas Choral Society, and Bach Society. Hot Springs hosts an opera workshop each summer, and Fort Smith supports a Little Theatre and a symphony orchestra.

Many of Arkansas's colleges have excellent music departments. The University of Arkansas's Schola Cantorum choral ensemble has an international reputation.

Folk- and country-music groups attract enthusiastic audiences as well. Mountain View's Ozark Folk Center presents authentic Ozark folk music. Eureka Spring's Ozark Mountain Hoe-Down is a delightful country-music show. The Arkansaw Traveller Folk and Dinner Theatre in Hardy presents a humorous blend of Ozark folklore and music.

Arkansas's literary tradition includes
noted writers Albert Pike (left), Opie Read
(center), and Ruth McEnery Stuart (right).

LITERATURE

One of Arkansas's earliest writers was soldier, lawyer,
newspaper editor, and poet Albert Pike. A native of Boston, Pike
arrived in Arkansas in 1832. Besides commanding a Confederate
brigade in the Civil War, he published hundreds of poems and
wrote a treatise on Masonic beliefs.

For better or worse, Arkansas's rugged, backwoods character
has captured the imaginations of many early writers. Stories with
Arkansas settings have been written by such famous authors as
O. Henry and Damon Runyan. Thomas Bangs Thorpe entertained
readers with such tales as "The Big Bear of Arkansas."

In the 1870s, newspaperman Opie Read wrote several novels on
Arkansas life and founded the weekly literary publication *The
Arkansaw Traveler*. Writers who worked in Arkansas in the late
1800s and early 1900s include Ruth McEnery Stuart, Alice French
(writing under the pen name Octave Thanet), George B. Rose, and
Charles J. Finger. Bernie Babcock, whose writing career began in

the 1920s, was known for her novels about Abraham Lincoln. Native authors Thyra Samter Winslow, David Thibault, and Charles Morrow Wilson earned literary success in the 1920s and 1930s.

More recently, folklorist Vance Randolph has published several collections of Ozark folk tales and legends. John Gould Fletcher's history of the state is full of picturesque anecdotes. Arkansas's notable writers today—some native-born and some from elsewhere—include Donald Harington, Mary Elsie Robertson, Lewis Nordan, and Dee Brown. Brown is perhaps best known for his novel *Bury My Heart at Wounded Knee*.

OUTDOOR RECREATION

A movement is underway in Arkansas to change the state nickname from Land of Opportunity to the Natural State. Residents and visitors alike find it easy to see why. Nature has blessed Arkansas with some of the most spectacular natural playgrounds in the country.

With more than 500,000 acres (more than 200,000 hectares) of lakes and 9,700 miles (15,600 kilometers) of rivers and streams, Arkansas is an ideal place for fishing, boating, waterskiing, canoeing, rafting, hiking, and camping. The exciting Buffalo National River in the Ozarks is a legend among the nation's canoeists and rafters.

Cutting through the south of Arkansas is the gentle, scenic Ouachita River. Dramatic bluffs and haunting forests line its banks. The White, Illinois, and Kings rivers and Lee and War Eagle creeks are other popular float streams. The White River is also known for its rainbow trout.

Almost all of Arkansas's lakes are reservoirs that were created

Arkansas's natural beauty and sparkling
rivers and lakes attract rock climbers
(left), boaters (bottom left), and fishing
enthusiasts (below, bottom right).

by the United States Army Corps of Engineers after World War II. Most are lined with parks and campsites. Along the Missouri border is massive Bull Shoals Lake, famous for its fine bass fishing. In the valleys of northwest Arkansas is Beaver Lake, which has 315 miles (507 kilometers) of shoreline. Greers Ferry Lake, edged by resorts and convention centers, features sailing regattas and an annual walleye fishing tournament. Lake Ouachita, near Hot Springs, lies within the rugged Ouachita National Forest. Other favorite spots are Norfork, De Gray, Greeson, and Dardanelle lakes.

Visitors to Arkansas's forty-four state parks can explore hidden mountain trails, tour mysterious swamps, camp along wooded shores, hunt for diamonds, or observe Ozark artisans practicing their trades. At Crater of Diamonds State Park, people can hunt for real diamonds in North America's only active diamond mine. Ozark artisans demonstrate their crafts at the Ozark Folk Center. Toltec Mounds, Prairie Grove Battlefield, Devil's Den, and Pinnacle Mountain are a few of Arkansas's other fascinating state parks.

Families enjoy visiting Arkansas's theme parks. These include Wild River Country in North Little Rock, Dogpatch U.S.A. near Harrison, Magic Springs Family Fun Park near Hot Springs, and Land of Kong near Eureka Springs.

TEAM SPORTS

A "wild bunch of razorback hogs" was what University of Arkansas football coach Hugo Bezdek called his team back in 1909. The name stuck, and the wildness caught on. Now thousands of Razorback fans don their hog hats for football season and go "hog-wild." Cheering their team on to victory, they roar a unique hog-call cheer, "Wooooo Pig SOOie!"

Left: Pinnacle Mountain State Park
Right: University of Arkansas football fans

The team truly rose to glory under Coach Frank Broyles.
Between 1958 and 1976, Broyles's Razorbacks racked up 144 wins
and 6 conference championships.

Arkansans are proud of their Razorback basketball team, too. In
1978, the team was one of the National College Athletic
Association's Final Four.

In the summer, thousands of fans and amateur basketball
players turn out for Little Rock's Hoop-D-Do Basketball
Tournament. One might even see Arkansas basketball heroes
Sidney Moncrief, Ron Brewer, or Marvin Delph on hand to inspire
the players.

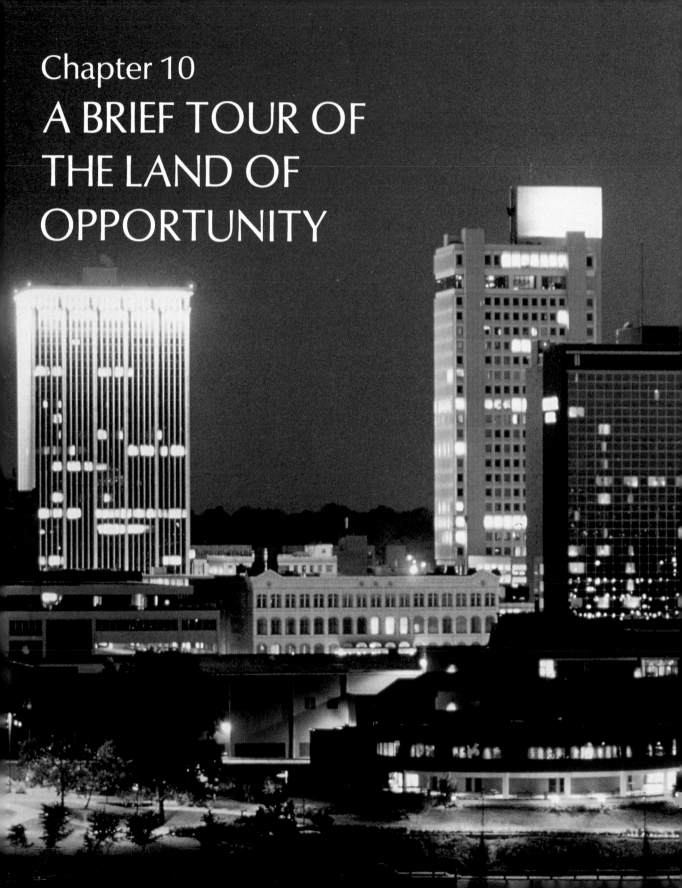

Chapter 10

A BRIEF TOUR OF
THE LAND OF
OPPORTUNITY

A BRIEF TOUR OF THE LAND OF OPPORTUNITY

THE HEART OF ARKANSAS

Called the Heart of Arkansas, Little Rock and the surrounding area offer a wealth of historical and recreational points of interest. Little Rock's ultramodern office buildings tower over the state's financial, political, and cultural center. Just as impressive is the city's historic legacy. The state capitol, at Capitol and Woodland streets, has been the state's seat of government since 1911. Built with limestone from Batesville, the capitol is a one-quarter-size replica of the United States Capitol in Washington, D.C. The chandelier in its rotunda, made by Tiffany & Company, weighs two tons.

On the north side of town, along the south bank of the Arkansas River, is Riverfront Park. This lovely city park is a pleasant place to take a stroll. Thousands flock to the park on Memorial Day weekend for entertainment, food, and fun at the annual Riverfest celebration.

At the north end of Rock Street, near the Union Pacific Railroad Bridge, is the Little Rock historical marker. This is the spot where Bénard de La Harpe first landed in 1722.

South of Riverfront Park is the historic section of downtown Little Rock, known as the Quapaw Quarter. Just beyond the park, facing Markham Street, is the Old State House. This gracious Greek Revival structure served as the state's original capitol building, from 1836 until 1911. Now a state-history museum, it

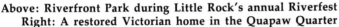

Above: Riverfront Park during Little Rock's annual Riverfest
Right: A restored Victorian home in the Quapaw Quarter

features the restored governor's office and legislative chambers, as well as Granny's Attic, a gallery of "touchable" items.

Next to the State House is Little Rock's major meeting center, the Statehouse Convention Center. Across Markham Street is the Capital Hotel, an elegantly restored 1877 hotel. Two blocks from the Old State House is Main Street. Several blocks of Main Street have been closed to traffic, forming the Metrocentre Mall. Here, the massive Main Street project—a renovation of five adjacent buildings into a spectacular mini-mall—is under way. Pedestrians enjoy strolling along the central walkway among newly designed stores, restaurants, and offices.

Nearby is the Arkansas Territorial Restoration. This indoor-and-outdoor museum features fourteen restored buildings from Arkansas's territorial period. One of these is the home and printing shop of William E. Woodruff, founder of the *Arkansas Gazette*.

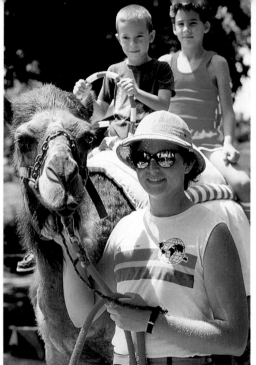

People of all ages enjoy the Little Rock Zoo.

A few blocks away is MacArthur Park, named for World War II hero General Douglas MacArthur. The park's Old Arsenal Building, where MacArthur was born, now houses the Museum of Science and History. Also in the park is the Arkansas Arts Center. The Arts Center includes the Pike-Fletcher-Terry Mansion, once the home of Albert Pike and now home of Little Rock's Decorative Arts Museum.

In War Memorial Park, west of the downtown area, is the Little Rock Zoo. This thirty-five-acre (fourteen-hectare) home for more than five hundred animals now includes a brand-new Great Ape Display. This facility houses the zoo's new pair of gorillas, as well as chimpanzees and orangutans.

Across the Arkansas River from Little Rock is North Little Rock, with its own Riverfront Park. The park's new Sesquicentennial Sundial is listed in the *Guinness Book of World Records* as the largest horizontal sundial in the world. Made with stones donated from all over the world, the sundial was built in 1986 to celebrate Arkansas's 150th birthday.

Pinnacle Mountain State Park is a wilderness area dominated by a volcano-shaped mountain.

Burns Park, farther north along the river, is the largest city park in Arkansas and the second largest in the country. Covering 1,600 acres (648 hectares), the park includes boat-launching ramps, hiking trails, and facilities for picnicking, camping, baseball, tennis, racquetball, and golf.

Just outside of the Little Rock and North Little Rock area are a number of interesting towns and recreation areas. To the west, near Roland, is Pinnacle Mountain State Park. This deeply forested park surrounds the rocky, cone-shaped peak of Pinnacle Mountain, where bird-watchers often spot gracefully soaring eagles.

At Benton, to the south, Hernando De Soto came upon salt deposits along the Saline River. A trail marker marks the spot where he and his men camped. Benton's Gann Building Museum, "the world's only bauxite house," is built entirely of blocks of Arkansas bauxite.

Claiming to be the "minnow capital of the world," Lonoke boasts the world's largest commercial minnow farm. The town presents its annual Minnow Madness festival every June. Jacksonville, to the northeast, is the home of Little Rock Air Force

Base. Thousands of guests attend the base's open house every October, during which they can tour gigantic aircraft and watch breathtaking air shows.

Northeast of Little Rock, along the Arkansas River near Conway, is Toad Suck Ferry Lock and Dam. The name dates to the 1800s, when the area was an important ferryboat landing with a nearby rivermen's saloon. According to local Indians, the patrons "sucked the bottle till they swelled up like toads." Now the surrounding park is an attractive riverside picnic and recreation area. Conway's annual Toad Suck Daze festival includes a Toad Jump-Off.

A short drive southeast of Little Rock is Toltec Mounds State Park. Here, amidst rolling fields of corn and wheat, are the remains of a prehistoric culture that flourished between A.D. 700 and 950. At the park's information center, visitors can see archaeological exhibits about the site. A tour along the park's trail reveals several impressive mounds and other earthen structures built in a plazalike arrangement.

WESTERN ARKANSAS

Fort Smith, an Arkansas River port on the Oklahoma border, was once the last outpost of American civilization. The original fort was established in 1817 to keep peace between warring Indians and to protect settlers from Indians and outlaws. Beyond this point lay the lawless stretches of Indian Territory. Today, Fort Smith National Historic Site, which includes the courtroom, jail, and gallows of Judge Isaac Parker, the "Hanging Judge," is one of the most visited spots in Arkansas.

The Belle Grove Historic District preserves the area where many of Fort Smith's military officers, steamboat captains, and

The Fort Smith Art Center is housed in a restored Victorian home in the Belle Grove Historic District.

politicians lived in the nineteenth century. Some of their ornate homes are now open to the public. Among them are the Clayton House and the building that is now the Fort Smith Arts Center.

In 1975, Fort Chaffee army base near Fort Smith served as America's largest Vietnamese refugee camp. Thousands of Cuban refugees occupied Fort Chaffee in 1980.

Rich farmland and many charming towns lie along the Arkansas River Valley between Fort Smith and Little Rock. Wiederkehr and Post wineries in Altus offer free winery tours and wine tastings. Visitors can also tour the pickle plant in Atkins. A few miles south of Atkins is the mountaintop state park of Petit Jean Mountain.

South of Paris is Magazine Mountain, the state's highest point. Farther south is the 1.5-million-acre (.6 million-hectare) Ouachita National Forest. Through the Ouachitas' forested sandstone hills winds Talimena Scenic Drive, which has many nature trails and picnic areas along the way. In Queen Wilhelmina State Park, one can enjoy cool mountain air and gorgeous scenery from the top of Rich Mountain.

The Hot Springs Fountain (left) in front of the visitor's center welcomes vacationers to Hot Springs, a resort famous for its hot-water health spas (center) and Thoroughbred horse racing (right).

The resort city of Hot Springs, east of the Ouachitas, is famous for its Thoroughbred horse racing and its hot-water health spas. Adults and children alike enjoy the city's Magic Springs theme park, Mid-America Museum, and Josephine Tussaud's Wax Museum.

SOUTHERN ARKANSAS

The southern part of Arkansas features swamplands, bayous (slow-moving streams), and forests of towering pines. Boating past mangroves or wandering through the pines, it is easy to imagine the prehistoric creatures whose remains have become southern Arkansas's fossil fuels.

In the 1920s, oil and natural gas were discovered in El Dorado and nearby Smackover. The Arkansas Oil and Brine Museum,

A family hunts for diamonds at Crater of Diamonds State Park.

between these two towns, tells the story of the area's oil-boom days. El Dorado is now an important commercial center for petroleum-related industries in southern Arkansas and northern Louisiana.

Crater of Diamonds State Park near Murfreesboro is situated on North America's only active diamond mine. It is also the only spot on the continent where the public is free to hunt for diamonds. More than sixty thousand of the precious gemstones have been found so far. The largest, nicknamed "Uncle Sam," weighed 40.42 carats.

The city of Texarkana, in the state's southwest corner, straddles the Arkansas-Texas border; there is a Texarkana in each state. Though legally two separate towns, each with its own city government and city services, the two Texarkanas function as one social and economic unit. The two cities are separated by an imaginary line down the center of State Line Avenue. The post

The town of Hope claims to be home of the world's largest watermelons.

office, which lies on the border and serves both cities, is officially located in "Texarkana, Arkansas-Texas."

Half an hour's drive from Texarkana is Washington, Arkansas's Confederate state capital during the Civil War. It was here that Sam Houston, Jim Bowie, Davy Crockett, and others plotted Texas's fight for independence from Mexico. Old Washington State Park preserves many historic sites and buildings from Washington's early days—including the blacksmith shop where the original "Bowie knife" was forged.

Only ten minutes from Washington is Hope, a town claiming to be home of the world's largest watermelons. Watermelon lovers flock to Hope's annual Watermelon Festival to compete in watermelon-eating and seed-spitting contests. Farmers vie for the biggest-watermelon prize, the winner usually weighing in at around two hundred pounds (ninety-one kilograms).

Farther east is Camden, which lies on the beautiful, scenic

In the Grand Prairie region, acres of emerald-colored rice shoots stretch as far as the eye can see.

Ouachita River. Camden's elegant McCollum-Chidester House served as headquarters for both Confederate and Union generals during the Civil War Battle of Poison Springs. The home's bullet scars remain as vivid reminders of the conflict. The battle site is now Poison Springs State Park, a peaceful maze of nature trails. Camden hosts an annual Great River Raft Race on the Ouachita River. Rules for the race are not strict; contestants race "anything that floats."

THE DELTA REGION

The region known as the Grand Prairie lies in southeastern Arkansas. Once cursed by farmers as useless swampland, the Grand Prairie is now the rice capital of the nation. Here, acres of emerald-colored rice shoots stretch as far as the eye can see.

The abundance of grain attracts dozens of species of waterfowl as they migrate along the route known as the Mississippi Flyway. Accordingly, residents also call the area the duck-hunting capital of the nation. The winter hunting season attracts droves of hunting enthusiasts, many of whom compete in an annual duck-calling contest.

The city of Stuttgart is the business center of the Grand Prairie region. Settled by German immigrants in the early 1900s, Stuttgart is now the home of Riceland Foods' gigantic food-processing complex.

Stuttgart is also home to the charming and fascinating Stuttgart Agricultural Museum. Outdoor exhibits include a small Grand Prairie village that features a schoolhouse, fire station, and newspaper shop. Inside are early steam tractors, threshing machines, and a 1930 Ford automobile. Displays show the history of rice farming in the area as well as early clothing and home furnishings. The museum's new waterfowl wing puts the visitor in the midst of the wetlands before sunrise. Lifelike models of dozens of waterfowl are accompanied by recordings of each one's unique call.

Southwest of Stuttgart is Pine Bluff, a major transportation hub for southeast Arkansas. Several rail routes pass through the city, and it is also an important Arkansas River port. Pine Bluff's architecture reflects both nineteenth- and twentieth-century styles. Lovely old homes along Barraque and Cherry streets recall the gracious elegance of the Old South. The modern Civic Center downtown was designed by noted architect Edward Durell Stone. The Civic Center's new International Peace Garden expresses Pine Bluff's harmonious relations with its adopted "sister city," Iwai City, Japan.

Along Arkansas's eastern border is a scenic parkway called the Great River Road. Pilot-wheel road signs mark historic sites along the way. Near the mouth of the Arkansas River is Arkansas Post National Memorial, site of the first European settlement in the lower Mississippi River Valley.

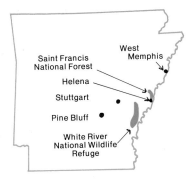

Pine Bluff is a major transportation hub for southeast Arkansas.

Farther north, past the White River National Wildlife Refuge, is Louisiana Purchase State Park. Here, in 1815, surveyors began marking off survey points for the Louisiana Purchase. A boardwalk runs through the park's thirty-seven acres (fifteen hectares) of headwater swamp. This area is a natural habitat for many unusual plants and animals.

Nearby Helena "occupies one of the prettiest situations on the river," according to Mark Twain. Perched on the bank of the Mississippi, Helena prospered in the days of the steamboats and later was the scene of several Civil War battles. Visitors can experience the charm of the Old South in elegant homes such as Estevan Hall, the Mosby House, and the Tappan Home.

Just north of Helena is the Saint Francis National Forest. Still farther north, at the intersection of Interstate highways 40 and 55, is West Memphis. More than a million people a year visit the city's Southland Greyhound Park, the largest greyhound race-track in the country.

Stretching north into Missouri is Crowley's Ridge, a long, narrow strip of hills noted for its yellow loess topsoil. Five state parks along the ridge offer campsites, fishing and swimming lakes, hiking trails, launch ramps, and playgrounds.

THE OZARKS

North of Little Rock the terrain rises steeply at the foothills of the Ozark Mountains. The Ozark National Forest covers much of northern and northwestern Arkansas. In this region, it is sometimes difficult to predict the travel time from one town to another, because the highways wind in a snakelike course up limestone hills and around ragged bluffs. Touring the Ozarks is worth the trouble, however. A visitor never forgets the glimpses of clear blue streams nestled in misty, blue-green valleys.

Boaters, water-skiers, swimmers, and fishing enthusiasts enjoy the Ozarks' four large artificially created lakes: Greers Ferry, Bull Shoals, Norfork, and Beaver. The spectacular Buffalo National River was the first in America to be declared a national river. Its limestone cliffs and treacherous rapids attract canoeists from all over the country.

State Highway 7 is known as one of the most scenic drives in America. From the Missouri border, it meanders down through the Ozarks and into the Arkansas River Valley and the Ouachita National Forest. Some of the attractions along Highway 7 include Bull Shoals Lake, the caverns near Harrison, Dogpatch U.S.A. amusement park, Alum Cove Natural Bridge, and the Ozark Highlands National Recreation Trail.

Mountain View, in north-central Arkansas, is the home of the Ozark Folk Center. Visitors here can watch Ozark artisans making candles, baskets, brooms, musical instruments, furniture, quilts, and many other items. In the 1,043-seat auditorium, musicians perform native Ozark tunes on Autoharps, dulcimers, banjos, and mandolins.

Northwest of Mountain View is Blanchard Springs Caverns. Visitors may take one of two tours, or trails, through these

The Ozarks offer such scenic wonders as Buffalo National River (above) and Blanchard Springs Caverns (right).

awesome calcite caves. The Dripstone Trail includes the magnificent Cathedral Room. The smaller Coral Room was called the cave find of the century when it was discovered in 1963. Hardier climbers may choose the Discovery Trail, which takes visitors deeper into the caverns.

In the northwest corner of the state, near Beaver Lake, is the charming Victorian town of Eureka Springs. An artists' colony since the 1930s, the town is built into the mountainside. Some streets seem to lead straight up into the air. Some buildings built on hillsides may be entered from the top floor, the bottom floor,

Eureka Springs is a charming town that features many carefully restored Victorian homes.

or points in between. Much of the downtown area is on the National Register of Historic Places.

Eureka Springs and the surrounding area offer a variety of attractions. The Ozark Mountain Hoe-Down and the Pine Mountain Jamboree present country music shows from March through December. Collectors enjoy Geuther's Doll Museum, Hammond Museum of Bells, and Miles Musical Museum. People come from all over the country to see the town's Great Passion Play. Outside of town, at the end of a wooded trail, stands Thorncrown Chapel. Built by noted architect E. Fay Jones, it is made almost entirely of glass.

Farther west along Highway 62 is Inspiration Point, a breathtaking overlook of the mountainsides and valleys below. Half an hour's drive away is Lost Bridge Village, which overlooks spectacular Beaver Lake. Continuing west, one arrives at Pea Ridge National Military Park, scene of the Civil War Battle of Pea Ridge.

Heading south toward Fayetteville, one passes the towns of Rogers and Springdale, whose tiny airports sport the sleek private jets of wealthy businessmen. Gigantic industries such as Wal-Mart and Tyson Foods are headquartered in this area.

In Fayetteville is the main campus of the University of Arkansas. Here one can see Old Main, the university's original building; Razorback Stadium, fondly called "Hog Heaven"; and the University Museum, which features archaeology and natural-history exhibits. The University Fine Arts Center was designed by architect Edward Durell Stone.

Fayetteville and its environs boast a number of historic points of interest. Fayetteville's Headquarters House served as headquarters for both Union and Confederate armies during the Civil War. Just west of town is the 130-acre (53-hectare) Prairie Grove Battlefield State Park, site of a major Civil War battle.

Weaving down Highway 71 out of the mountains, with scenic vistas around every bend, a traveler can see why Arkansas has been called the Wonder State and the Natural State. This traveler has truly seen a Land of Opportunity for artists, adventurers, and all who love the land.

FACTS AT A GLANCE

GENERAL INFORMATION

Statehood: June 25, 1836, twenty-fifth state

Origin of Name: The word *Arkansas* was one of the early French translations of the Indian word *Ugaxpa*, which means "downstream people" and referred to the Quapaw Indians.

State Capital: Little Rock, founded 1821

State Nickname: "Land of Opportunity" has been the official state nickname since 1953; "Wonder State" was the official nickname from 1923 to 1953.

State Flag: Arkansas's state flag was adopted in 1913. It features a blue-bordered white diamond on a field of red. The diamond indicates that Arkansas is the nation's only diamond-producing state. Twenty-five white stars within the blue border represent Arkansas's place as the twenty-fifth state to enter the Union. In the center of the diamond is the word *Arkansas,* with one blue star above it and three blue stars below. The three stars beneath the state name represent Arkansas's historical allegiance to Spain, France, and the United States. The single star above the name represents the Confederacy.

State Motto: *Regnat Populus,* a Latin phrase meaning "the people rule"

State Bird: Mockingbird

State Flower: Apple blossom

State Tree: Pine tree

State Insect: Honeybee

State Gem: Diamond

State Beverage: Milk

State Musical Instrument: Fiddle

State Fruit: South Arkansas vine-ripened pink tomato

State Song: "Arkansas," words and music by Eva Ware Barnett, adopted as the official state song in 1963:

I am thinking tonight of the Southland,
Of the home of my childhood days,
Where I roamed through the woods and the meadows,
By the mill and the brook that plays;
Where the roses are in bloom,
And the sweet magnolia too,
Where the jasmine is white,
And the fields are violet blue,
There a welcome awaits all her children
Who have wandered afar from home.

Chorus:
Arkansas, Arkansas, 'tis a name dear,
'Tis the place I call "Home, Sweet Home";
Arkansas, Arkansas, I salute thee,
From thy shelter no more I'll roam.
'Tis a land full of joy and of sunshine
Rich in pearls and in diamonds rare.
Full of hope, faith and love for the stranger
Who may pass 'neath her portals fair;
There the rice fields are full,
And the cotton, corn and hay,
There the fruits of the field bloom in winter months and May,
'Tis the land that I love,
First of all dear,
And to her let us all give cheer.

POPULATION

Population: 2,286,419, thirty-third among the states (1980 census)

Population Density: 43 people per sq. mi. (17 people per km²)

Population Distribution: 52 percent of the people live in cities or towns. More than 17 percent live in the Little Rock metropolitan area.

Little Rock	158,915
Fort Smith	71,626
North Little Rock	64,388
Pine Bluff	56,636
Fayetteville	36,608
Hot Springs	35,781

(Population figures according to 1980 census)

Population Growth: Arkansas's population grew tremendously during its territorial days in the early 1800s and throughout the nineteenth century. In the early twentieth century, the population continued to increase, though more slowly than before. The number of residents declined during the 1940s and 1950s as people left the state to seek better jobs. However, from 1970 to 1980, this trend has reversed dramatically—the state's population grew almost 19 percent. During the same decade, the population of the United States as a whole grew 11.45 percent. The list below shows Arkansas's population growth since 1820:

Year	Population
1820	14,273
1840	97,574
1860	435,450
1880	802,525
1900	1,311,564
1920	1,752,204
1940	1,949,387
1950	1,909,511
1960	1,786,272
1970	1,923,322
1980	2,286,419

GEOGRAPHY

Borders: States that border Arkansas are Missouri on the north, Tennessee and Mississippi on the east, Louisiana on the south, Texas on the southwest, and Oklahoma on the west.

Highest Point: Magazine Mountain, 2,753 ft. (839 m)

Lowest Point: On the Ouachita River in Ashley and Union counties, 55 ft. (17 m)

Greatest Distances: North to south—240 mi. (386 km)
East to west—275 mi. (443 km)

Area: 53,187 sq. mi. (137,754 km²)

Rank in Area Among the States: Twenty-seventh

Rivers: The Mississippi River forms most of Arkansas's eastern border. The waters of all of Arkansas's rivers eventually empty into the Mississippi River. The Arkansas River, a major tributary of the Mississippi, flows across the state from northwest to southeast. The McClellan-Kerr Arkansas River Navigation System, opened in 1971, stabilized the Arkansas River's banks and widened channels to improve navigation. Other major rivers in Arkansas are the Ouachita River in the south, the White River in the north and east, the Saint Francis River in the east, and

Crappie fishing at night on Bull Shoals Lake in the Ozarks

the Red River in the southwest. The Buffalo River in the Ozarks has been designated a national river by Congress. The Saline River, named for its salt deposits, flows south from central Arkansas. Other rivers in Arkansas include the Black, Little Missouri, Kings, and Caddo rivers.

Lakes: Most of Arkansas's lakes were artificially created by the United States Army Corps of Engineers after World War II. Made by damming rivers, these lakes provide flood control, hydroelectric power, and recreational opportunities. Along the White River in the northern Ozarks region are Bull Shoals, Beaver, and Norfork lakes. In the Ouachita Mountains are Lakes Ouachita, Hamilton, and Catherine. Other large Arkansas lakes include Greers Ferry, Felsenthal, Greeson, De Gray, Millwood, Fort Smith, Nimrod, and Big Maumelle. The state's largest naturally occurring lake is Lake Chicot, in the southeast part of the state near the Mississippi River. It is an "oxbow" lake, formed by a change in the Mississippi River's course.

Springs: In and around Arkansas's Ozark and Ouachita mountain regions are a number of natural springs. Mammoth Spring, in the Ozarks, is one of the largest in the country. It yields about 235 million gal. (890 million l) of water a day. Eureka Springs, also in the Ozarks, has about sixty-five springs. Hot Springs, in the Ouachita region, is known for its forty-seven hot mineral springs. Discovered by Hernando De Soto in 1541, these springs are now a major attraction of this resort community.

Topography: Arkansas's major geographical regions can be divided into the highlands of the north and west and the lowlands of the south and east.

Arkansas's highlands include three topographic regions. The Ozark Plateau in the north reaches into the state from southern Missouri and includes the high tablelands and deep valleys of the Ozark Mountains. Along the southern edge of the Ozarks are the rugged Boston Mountains. In the west, extending into Oklahoma, are the east-west ridges of the Ouachita Mountains. Between the Ozarks and the Ouachitas lies the fertile Arkansas River Valley.

Arkansas's lowlands can be divided into two topographic regions. A wide band of land lying along the Mississippi River in the east is part of the Mississippi Alluvial Plain. In the northeastern part of this region, stretching into Missouri, is a strip of hills called Crowley's Ridge. The Grand Prairie, in the southeastern part of the Mississippi Alluvial Plain, was once a vast swampland but is now a fertile rice-

Arkansas moonrise

growing region. The south-central and southwestern part of the state lies in the West Gulf Coastal Plain. This region features pine-forested hills as well as swamps and bayous (slow-moving streams).

Climate: Arkansas's climate is generally warm and humid, with hot summers and mild winters. Temperatures in the northern and western highlands are generally lower than those in the southern and eastern lowlands. The average July temperature in northwest Arkansas is 79° F. (26° C); July temperatures in the southeast average 83° F. (28° C). In January, the northwest's average temperature is 39° F. (4° C); the southeast averages 45° F. (7° C). The town of Ozark registered the state's highest recorded temperature, 120° F. (49° C), on August 10, 1936. Pond set the record for the state's lowest temperature, -29° F. (-34° C), on February 13, 1905. Most of Arkansas's precipitation comes in the form of rain. On the average, the state receives about 49 in. (124 cm) of precipitation a year. Snowfall in Arkansas occurs mainly in the highlands and averages about 6 in. (15 cm) a year. Snow is rarely seen in some parts of the south and east.

NATURE

Trees: About half of Arkansas's land area is covered with forest. Both pines and hardwoods grow in the Ozark and Ouachita mountains. In the southern forests are loblolly and shortleaf pines. Other types of trees found in the state are oak, elm,

The three-toed box turtle is one of the many reptiles that can be found in Arkansas.

ash, hickory, gum, buckeye, basswood, pecan, hawthorn, cypress, water oak, holly, tulip (yellow poplar), mimosa, redbud, dogwood, red haw, crab apple, wild plum, locust, smoke tree, mulberry, fringe tree, and wax myrtle.

Wild Plants: Black-eyed Susan, passionflower, water lily, American bellflower, several kinds of orchids, butterfly weed, blue lobelia, verbena, phlox, yellow jasmine, hibiscus, aster, azalea, and wild hydrangea are among the flowers found in Arkansas. The fern *Woodsia scopulina*, found on Magazine Mountain, grows nowhere else between the Appalachians and the Rocky Mountains.

Animals: Throughout Arkansas are rabbits, squirrels, opossums, raccoons, weasels, woodchucks, skunks, and muskrats. Deer, red foxes, and bobcats roam the forests. Black bears, which had been nearly eliminated by overhunting, have been reintroduced by the Game and Fish Commission. Armadillos have spread into Arkansas from the southwestern United States and are seen even high in the Ozarks. Several species of turtles, lizards, and frogs inhabit the state. Arkansas's poisonous snakes include water moccasins, rattlesnakes, copperheads, and coral snakes. Nonpoisonous species include king snakes, garter snakes, and blue racers.

Birds: More than three hundred kinds of birds can be found in Arkansas, including blue jays, mockingbirds, robins, nuthatches, painted buntings, brown thrashers, and several species of sparrows and woodpeckers. A law protects the red-headed woodpecker. Whippoorwills, phoebes, and goldfinches are found in the mountains, while cranes and blue herons are seen around rivers in the lowlands. In the fall, the rice fields of the Grand Prairie attract many kinds of wild ducks and geese, as well as woodcocks, pheasants, and quails.

Fish: In Arkansas's rivers and lakes there are rainbow trout, bream, crappie, perch, carp, buffalofish, catfish, and several kinds of bass.

The state capitol at Christmastime

GOVERNMENT

Arkansas has had five state constitutions since it became a state in 1836. The 1836 constitution remained in effect until 1861. New constitutions were adopted in 1864 and 1868. Finally, in 1874, the constitution that is in effect today was adopted.

Arkansas's state government is structured in the same way as the federal government. There are three branches of state government: the legislative, which makes state laws; the executive, which enforces the laws; and the judicial, which interprets the laws. The Arkansas state legislature, or General Assembly, consists of two houses: a senate and a house of representatives. Arkansas's thirty-five senators are elected to four-year terms. The one hundred members of the house of representatives come from the state's eighty-four congressional districts. They are elected to two-year terms. Regular sessions of the General Assembly convene on the second Monday of January in odd-numbered years and usually last up to sixty business days. In addition, the governor may call special sessions.

The governor is the state's chief executive. Other executive officers are the lieutenant governor, secretary of state, attorney general, treasurer, auditor, and land commissioner. All are elected to four-year terms and may be reelected any number of times. The governor appoints other state officers; many of these appointments must be approved by the state senate.

The state supreme court is the highest court in the state's judicial system. Its chief justice and six associate justices are elected to eight-year terms. Voters from the state's twenty circuit-court districts elect circuit-court judges to four-year terms. These judges handle civil and criminal cases and hear appeals from lower courts. Chancery judges in the twenty chancery-court districts are elected to six-year terms. They preside over "equity" matters, such as mortgages and domestic relations. Arkansas also has county, municipal, and justice-of-the-peace courts.

In Arkansas, the basic unit of government is the county. County judges preside over county business and county courts. Other county officers include the sheriff, tax assessor, county clerk, treasurer, surveyor, coroner, and tax collector (a position sometimes held by the sheriff). Most cities and towns are governed by a mayor and a city council. Some, such as Little Rock, have the city council-manager form of government.

Number of Counties: 75

U.S. Representatives: 4

Electoral Votes: 6

Voting Qualifications: Eighteen years of age, state resident for twelve months, county resident for six months, district resident for one month

EDUCATION

In 1819, Arkansas's territorial legislature set aside every sixteenth section of public land for educational use. Dwight Mission, near Russellville, was the first school in Arkansas Territory. It was founded in 1820 by Reverend Cephas Washburn to teach Cherokee children in the area. In 1843, the state legislature established a public-school system. However, by 1860 there were only twenty-five public schools in Arkansas, and many parents were sending their children to private academies. After 1864, the Freedmen's Bureau began opening schools for black children. The state constitutions of 1868 and 1874 set up a statewide system of free education. Beginning in 1909, public-school attendance was required for all children between the ages of eight and fifteen. Today, children between the ages of six and fifteen are required to attend school. The state began providing free textbooks in 1937. Little Rock's public high schools were closed in 1958 in reaction to national racial integration requirements. However, they reopened the following year to admit both black and white students. By 1966, all of the state's public schools were desegregated.

Seventy-five percent of Arkansas's students graduate from high school, compared to 71 percent in the nation as a whole. Arkansas high-school students rank high academically. Their average combined Scholastic Aptitude Test (SAT) score is 999, compared to the national average of 893.

Of Arkansas's fourteen accredited colleges and universities, the largest is the University of Arkansas, founded in 1871. Its main campus is in Fayetteville, and branch campuses are located in Little Rock, Pine Bluff, and Monticello. On the Little Rock campus is the University of Arkansas Medical Center. Arkansas's oldest college, founded in 1836, is Arkansas College in Batesville. Some of the state's other institutions of higher learning are Arkansas State University, in Jonesboro; Arkansas Tech University, in Russellville; the University of Central Arkansas and Hendrix College, both in Conway; Henderson State University and Ouachita Baptist University, both in Arkadelphia; Southern Arkansas University, in Magnolia; Southern Baptist College, in Walnut Ridge; and Harding University, in Searcy.

A father and son harvesting grapes in Altus

ECONOMY AND INDUSTRY

Principal Products:
Agriculture: Broilers, soybeans, rice, wheat, cotton, eggs, milk, beef cattle, turkeys, sorghum grain, cottonseed, hogs, oats, hay, corn, grasses, grapes, snap beans, tomatoes, pecans, strawberries, dairy products
Manufacturing: Food products, electrical machinery and equipment, lumber and wood products, paper products, fabricated metal products, chemicals, non-electrical machinery, rubber and plastic products, printed materials, transportation equipment
Natural Resources: Water, soil, pine and hardwood timber, coal, petroleum, natural gas and natural gas liquids, bauxite, barite, bromine, clay, diamonds, granite, gypsum, lignite, limestone, marble, mercury, sand and gravel, vanadium

Business and Trade: Service industries account for nearly two-thirds of Arkansas's gross state product. Of these industries, wholesale and retail trade are the most important. Almost one-fourth of Arkansas's gross state product comes from manufacturing. Food processing is the major manufacturing activity; electrical equipment and wood products are next in importance. The wholesale trade of farm products and processed foods is centered mainly in Little Rock, and many wood products are wholesaled in Fort Smith. Riceland Foods, Tyson Foods, Wal-Mart Stores, Dillard Department Stores, Murphy Oil, and Stephens, Inc. are among Arkansas's major locally based corporations.

Communication: About thirty daily and sixty weekly newspapers are published in Arkansas. The *Arkansas Gazette* and the *Arkansas Democrat*, both published in

Little Rock, are the state's most important newspapers. Founded in 1819, the *Arkansas Gazette* is the oldest continuously published newspaper west of the Mississippi River. Other major newspapers are Fort Smith's *Southwest Times Record* and Texarkana's *Gazette*.

About 150 radio stations broadcast from Arkansas's cities and towns. The state's first radio station was Pine Bluff's WOK, which began broadcasting in 1921. Arkansas's first commercial television station was Little Rock's KATV, which began operation in 1953. Today the state has about 15 commercial television stations.

Transportation: The Grand Prairie Trace, between Little Rock and Brinkley, was one of Arkansas's earliest land trails. Arkansas's rivers also provided transportation for early settlers. Goods were transported by flatboats and keelboats that traveled down the Arkansas River and its tributaries to the Mississippi River. Mississippi steamboats began to appear on the Arkansas River in the 1820s. The California Gold Rush of 1849 boosted the state's transportation facilities, as many gold seekers used Arkansas as a major supply point on their westward journey. By the 1860s, railroads had replaced steamboats as the major commercial carriers. The railroads expanded and flourished until about 1910. Since then, railroad mileage has decreased.

Today, Arkansas's four major rail systems run on about 3,600 mi. (5,800 km) of track. Since the opening of the McClellan-Kerr Arkansas River Navigation System in 1971, the Arkansas River has once again become a major commercial navigation route. The system includes seventeen locks and dams, with major commercial ports at Pine Bluff, Little Rock, and Fort Smith. Osceola and Helena have ports along the Mississippi River. Camden has a port on the Ouachita River.

Arkansas has a total of about 77,000 mi. (124,000 km) of paved roadways, including federal and state highways and county roads. Many of the state's major highways intersect in Little Rock. Interstate 40 is an east-west route across the state. It replaces Route 66, the highway that once ran all the way across the country from the Atlantic Ocean to the Pacific Ocean. Interstate 30 connects Little Rock and the southwest city of Texarkana before it continues into Texas. In the east, West Memphis marks the southern end of Interstate 55, which runs north to St. Louis, Missouri, and Chicago, Illinois. Along the Mississippi River is a network of highways called the Great River Road. Green-and-white pilot-wheel signs mark historical points of interest along the way.

Forty of Arkansas's eighty-six commercial airports are equipped to handle large business jets. Little Rock's airport is the largest in the state, offering service from the nation's major passenger and freight airlines. Commuter airlines serve many of the state's smaller cities and towns.

SOCIAL AND CULTURAL LIFE

Museums: Little Rock, the state's capital and largest city, has many fine museums. Among them is the Arkansas Territorial Restoration, a collection of fourteen restored historic buildings from Arkansas's territorial days. The city's Old State House, once the state capitol, now houses a state-history museum. In MacArthur Park is the Arkansas Arts Center and the Old Arsenal Building, which

A spring garden (left) and a weaving demonstration (above) at the Arkansas Territorial Restoration in Little Rock

now houses the Museum of Science and History. The nearby Pike-Fletcher-Terry House, once owned by Albert Pike, is now the home of the Decorative Arts Museum.

In Fayetteville, the University of Arkansas Museum displays historical, archaeological, and mineral exhibits. Fort Smith's Old Fort Museum features historical artifacts from the days of Judge Isaac Parker, whose courtroom and gallows are nearby. Mound Builder artifacts can be seen in Wilson's Hampson Museum, while Quapaw relics are displayed in Pine Bluff's Jefferson County Historical Museum. Berryville's Saunders Museum features firearms of famous outlaws, and Rogers's Daisy International Air Gun Museum has the world's largest collection of air rifles. Some of Arkansas's other fascinating museums are the Arkansas State University Museum in Jonesboro, the Arkansas Agricultural Museum in Stuttgart, the Southeast Arkansas Arts and Science Center in Pine Bluff, the Arkansas Oil and Brine Museum in Smackover, Mid-America Center and Read's Museum of Automobiles in Hot Springs, Phillips County Museum in Helena, and Miles Musical Museum in Eureka Springs.

Libraries: William Woodruff, who founded the *Arkansas Gazette*, established the state's first lending library in Little Rock in 1843. Members who donated money to the library were allowed to use its books. The Helena Public Library, which opened in 1888, became the state's first tax-supported library in 1911. A statewide public library system was established in 1935, when the state legislature instituted the Arkansas Library Commission. Now there are about fifteen county libraries, fifteen regional libraries, and many city libraries throughout the state. Including the books in its Fayetteville and Little Rock campus libraries, the University of Arkansas owns the largest collection of books in the state.

A production at the Arkansas Repertory Theatre in Little Rock

Performing Arts: Among Little Rock's performing arts ensembles are the Arkansas Symphony Orchestra, the Arkansas Repertory Theatre, the Arkansas Opera Theatre, the Arkansas Choral Society, and the Bach Society. Several cities and towns support local orchestras and other performance groups. Fort Smith and Pine Bluff each have a symphony orchestra and theater groups. Hot Springs holds an opera workshop every summer. The University of Arkansas has a strong music department.

Folk and country music enjoy a wide following in Arkansas. Authentic traditional Ozark folk music, featuring instruments such as the dulcimer, mandolin, Autoharp, fiddle, and Dobro, is performed at the Ozark Folk Center in Mountain View. Country music shows can be seen at Eureka Spring's Ozark Mountain Hoe-Down and Pine Mountain Jamboree, Hardy's Arkansaw Traveller Folk and Dinner Theatre, and in many other communities. Blues can be heard in the Delta region and some other parts of the state. Bluegrass, country-western, and country rock are some of Arkansas's other popular musical styles.

Sports and Recreation: Arkansas is an ideal state for outdoor recreation. It has more than 500,000 acres (more than 200,000 hectares) of lakes and some 9,700 mi. (15,600 km) of rivers and streams, and about half the state is covered with forestland. People who enjoy the outdoors find many opportunities for fishing, hunting, boating, waterskiing, canoeing, rafting, hiking, and camping in Arkansas. The Buffalo National River is popular among float-trippers throughout the country. Other favorite float streams are the Ouachita, White, Illinois, and Kings rivers and Lee and War Eagle creeks.

Arkansas's lakes, most of them artificially created, also provide many recreational opportunities. The largest, high in the Ozarks, is Bull Shoals Lake. Beaver Lake, also in the Ozarks, opens up into several valleys of the White River. Felsenthal Lake in the south is surrounded by a large wildlife refuge. Other popular lakes are Greers Ferry, Ouachita, Norfork, De Gray, Greeson, Fort Smith, Maumelle, and Dardanelle.

Cedar Falls at Petit Jean State Park in central Arkansas

Arkansas's forty-four state parks include Toltec Mounds, a prehistoric Indian-mound site; Ozark Folk Center, where Ozark artisans demonstrate their crafts; Pinnacle Mountain, a cone-shaped peak with a stunning view; and Crater of Diamonds, where the public may hunt for diamonds. Popular family theme parks are Wild River Country in North Little Rock, Dogpatch U.S.A. near Harrison, and Magic Springs Family Fun Park near Hot Springs.

During football season, Arkansans rally around the Razorbacks, the University of Arkansas football team. From 1958 to 1976, under Coach Frank Broyles, the team won 144 games and 6 conference championships.

Historic Sites and Landmarks:

Arkansas Post National Memorial, near Gillett, is the site of the first permanent European settlement in the lower Mississippi River Valley, founded by Henri de Tonti in 1686. From 1819 to 1821, it served as Arkansas's first territorial capital.

Fort Smith National Historic Site, in Fort Smith, was one of the first United States military posts in the Louisiana Territory. Among the officers who served there were Zachary Taylor, later president of the United States; and Jefferson Davis, later president of the Confederacy. The courtroom, jail, and gallows of Judge Isaac Parker, the "Hanging Judge," are also featured at the site. Between 1875 and 1896, Judge Parker sentenced 177 men to the gallows (88 of whom were actually executed) from his Fort Smith courtroom.

A reenactment of the Battle of Prairie Grove at Prairie Grove Battlefield State Park

Pea Ridge National Military Park, in Pea Ridge, is the site of a Civil War battle that involved more than twenty-six thousand troops.

Prairie Grove Battlefield State Park, in Prairie Grove, is the site of the Civil War Battle of Prairie Grove. The park includes a reconstructed nineteenth-century village and a museum that describes the life of a Civil War soldier.

Toltec Mounds State Park, near England, preserves the remains of a large ceremonial complex that was built between A.D. 700 and 950 by people of the Plum Bayou Culture.

Other Interesting Places to Visit:

Arkansas Agricultural Museum, in Stuttgart, features a small Grand Prairie village, as well as steam-powered tractors, displays on the history of rice farming in the area, and true-to-life waterfowl exhibits.

Arkansas Territorial Restoration, in Little Rock, features fourteen historic buildings from Arkansas's territorial days.

Blanchard Springs Caverns, near Mountain View, feature magnificent calcite stalactites and stalagmites, as well as many other cave features. The Discovery Trail at the caverns takes visitors through huge cave rooms, past water-carved passages, and along a cave stream.

Buffalo National River, the nation's first national river, winds for 132 mi. (212 km) through the Ozarks. It is famous among canoeists for its rapids, waterfalls, and sinkholes, as well as for its massive cliffs, scenic canyons and valleys, and surrounding forests and caves.

Crater of Diamonds State Park, near Murfreesboro, is the site of the only active diamond mine in North America. The general public may hunt for diamonds in the park and keep whatever they find. So far, visitors have found more than sixty thousand diamonds.

Eureka Springs, an artists' colony in the northwest Ozarks, is a Victorian town built into the mountainside. Much of the downtown area is on the National Register of Historic Places.

Hot Springs National Park, in Hot Springs, is a health-spa and resort area that features hot mineral-spring waters. Yielding about 1 million gal. (3.8 million l) of water a day, the spring waters have an average temperature of 143° F. (62° C). Several historic bathhouses in the area are being renovated.

Ozark Folk Center, in Mountain View, is dedicated to preserving native Ozark folk crafts and folk music. Visitors can attend authentic folk-music performances, and can watch blacksmiths, potters, candle makers, weavers, and many other craftspeople practicing their trades.

IMPORTANT DATES

c. 10,000 B.C.—Paleo-Indians first inhabit Arkansas

A.D. 700 to 950—Plum Bayou Culture flourishes in central Arkansas

1541—Hernando De Soto crosses the Mississippi River into Arkansas and leads an expedition through the region

1673—Father Jacques Marquette and Louis Jolliet explore the Mississippi River, traveling south as far as the mouth of the Arkansas River

1682—René-Robert Cavelier, Sieur de La Salle, explores the Mississippi River all the way to its mouth at the Gulf of Mexico; he claims all the Mississippi River Valley, including Arkansas, for France and names the region Louisiana

1686—Henri de Tonti establishes Arkansas Post, the first permanent white settlement in the lower Mississippi River Valley

An eighteenth-century caricature of Scottish financier John Law, who attempted to colonize the Arkansas region in 1717

1687 — Survivors of La Salle's expedition travel from Texas across southern and southeastern Arkansas to Arkansas Post

1717 — Scottish financier John Law persuades the French government to allow him to establish a European settlement near Arkansas Post

1721 — John Law's plan to colonize the Louisiana territory fails; many settlers abandon the settlement in the Arkansas region

1722 — French explorer Bénard de La Harpe leads an expedition from New Orleans up the Mississippi and Arkansas rivers; about 150 mi. (241 km) inland from Arkansas Post he spots the outcropping of rock that eventually becomes known as the Little Rock

1763 — After the French and Indian War, France cedes its lands west of the Mississippi (the territory of Louisiana), including the land of present-day Arkansas, to Spain

1800 — By the secret Treaty of San Ildefonso, Spain cedes Louisiana back to France

1803 — The United States purchases Louisiana from France, making the land of present-day Arkansas part of the United States

1806 — The District of Arkansas is created within the Louisiana Territory

1812 — The southern part of the Louisiana Territory becomes the state of Louisiana; the northern part, including present-day Arkansas, becomes the Missouri Territory

1815 — United States government surveyors establish a base point near Marianna for surveying the Louisiana Purchase lands

1817 — The military post of Fort Smith is established

1819 — Arkansas Territory is established, with its capital at Arkansas Post and with General James Miller as territorial governor; William Woodruff begins publishing the *Arkansas Gazette* at Arkansas Post

1820 — The Reverend Cephas Washburn sets up Dwight Mission, Arkansas's first school

1821 — The capital of Arkansas Territory is moved to Little Rock

1836 — Arkansas is admitted to the Union as the twenty-fifth state

1843 — The state legislature establishes a public-school system

1847 — Former Arkansas governor Archibald Yell leads a regiment of Arkansas volunteers in the Battle of Buena Vista during the Mexican War

1849 — During the California Gold Rush, Fort Smith and Van Buren become supply bases for those traveling to the western goldfields

1853 — Arkansas's first railroad company is organized

1861 — Arkansas secedes from the Union and joins the Confederate States of America

1862 — Union army forces defeat Confederate forces at the Battle of Pea Ridge; the Confederates win the Battle of Prairie Grove but later surrender their stand

1863 — Little Rock is captured by Union forces; Arkansas's Confederate state capital is moved to Washington in Hempstead County, with Harris Flanagin as governor

1864 — A Union state government is set up in Little Rock, with Isaac Murphy as governor

1865 — The Civil War ends; Arkansas's Confederate state government surrenders to the Union

1868 — Arkansas is readmitted to the Union; northern Republicans reorganize the state government as Reconstruction begins

1871 — Arkansas Industrial University (now the University of Arkansas) is founded in Fayetteville

1874—Reconstruction period ends; Arkansas adopts its present state constitution; the Brooks-Baxter War divides Republicans throughout Arkansas and paves the way for the return of Democratic rule of the state

1901—Natural gas is discovered near Fort Smith

1906—Diamond deposits are discovered near Murfreesboro

1907—Ouachita National Forest is established

1908—Ozark National Forest is established

1911—The Arkansas legislature begins meeting in Little Rock's new state capitol

1921—Arkansas's first oil well is drilled near El Dorado

1923—The Wonder State becomes Arkansas's official nickname

1927—The Mississippi and Arkansas rivers overflow, causing the worst flood in the state's history

1928—Arkansas senator Joe T. Robinson runs for vice-president with Democratic presidential candidate Al Smith

1932—Arkansan Hattie Caraway becomes the nation's first woman to be elected to the United States Senate

1953—Arkansas's official nickname is changed to Land of Opportunity

1955—The Arkansas Industrial Development Commission (AIDC) is established to develop the state's industrial potential

1957—President Eisenhower sends federal troops to Little Rock to desegregate Little Rock Central High School

1958—To halt desegregation, Governor Orval Faubus refuses to allow Arkansas's public high schools to open for the 1958-59 school year

1959—Arkansas's public high schools reopen on an integrated basis

1964—Governor Orval Faubus becomes the first Arkansas governor to be elected to a sixth term

1966—Winthrop Rockefeller becomes Arkansas's first Republican governor since Reconstruction days

1970—The McClellan-Kerr Arkansas River Navigation System is completed, providing river navigation from Oklahoma through Arkansas to the Mississippi River

1980 — Arkansans vote against adopting a new state constitution

1983 — The state legislature approves sweeping school-reform measures sponsored by Governor Bill Clinton

1986 — Arkansas celebrates its sesquicentennial

1989 — Based on Arkanas's progress in improving education, Governor Bill Clinton serves as the lead governor in President Bush's Education Summit, which drafts national education goals

IMPORTANT PEOPLE

Maya Angelou (1928-   ), born Marguerite Johnson; grew up in Stamps; poet, playwright, editor, and educator; best-known work is the novel *I Know Why the Caged Bird Sings*

Katherine Susan Anthony (1877-1965), born in Roseville; writer; author of *Feminism in Germany and Scandinavia* and several biographies of famous women, including *Catherine the Great, Queen Elizabeth, Marie Antoinette,* and *Louisa May Alcott*

Bernie Babcock (1868-1962), writer; known for her novels about Abraham Lincoln; moved to Arkansas as a young woman and supported the prohibition and feminist movements; founded Little Rock's Arkansas Museum of Science and History

Benjamin Louis Eulalie de Bonneville (1795-1878), French-born soldier and adventurer; explored America's Northwest Territory (1832-35); appointed commander of the post at Fort Smith in 1838; became a brigadier general on the Union side in the Civil War; retired to Fort Smith in 1871; was the subject of Washington Irving's *The Adventures of Captain Bonneville*

Dee Alexander Brown (1908-   ), grew up in Stephens and Little Rock; writer, historian, and librarian; has written numerous Western-history novels; best known for *Bury My Heart at Wounded Knee*

Frank Broyles (1924-   ), coach of the University of Arkansas Razorbacks football team (1958-76); led the team to 144 victories and 6 conference championships

Bob Burns (1890-1956), born in Greenwood; entertainer; popular radio comedian in the 1930s

Glen Campbell (1938-   ), born in Delight; country and pop singer, entertainer

Hattie Ophelia Wyatt Caraway (1878-1950), politician; first woman ever elected to the U.S. Senate; appointed to complete the term of her husband, Arkansas Senator Thaddeus Caraway, when he died in 1931; elected to the Senate in her own right (1932-45); became the first woman to head a Senate committee and the first woman to preside over a session of the U.S. Senate

MAYA ANGELOU

GLEN CAMPBELL

HATTIE CARAWAY

ELDRIDGE CLEAVER

DIZZY DEAN

ORVAL FAUBUS

JAMES FULBRIGHT

James Paul Clarke (1854-1916), politician; U.S. senator from Arkansas (1903-16); served as president *pro tempore* of the Senate (1913); governor of Arkansas (1895-97); championed strict regulation of railroads; his statue stands in Statuary Hall in the U.S. Capitol in Washington, D.C.

Leroy (Eldridge) Cleaver (1935-   ), born in Wabbaseka; civil-rights activist; Black Panther party leader; felt that blacks needed to organize politically to make progress in American society; best known for his book *Soul on Ice*

Jeff Davis (1862-1913), born in Little River County; politician; leader of the Agrarian Revolt in Arkansas; championed the common man and opposed big business; governor of Arkansas (1901-07); U.S. senator (1907-13)

Jay Hanna "Dizzy" Dean (1911-1974), born in Lucas; professional baseball player; one of baseball's greatest pitchers; pitched for the St. Louis Cardinals (1932-37) and the Chicago Cubs (1938-41); pitched thirty winning games in 1934; elected to the National Baseball Hall of Fame (1953)

Orval Eugene Faubus (1910-   ), born near Combs; politician; governor of Arkansas (1955-67); only Arkansas governor to serve six consecutive terms; remembered for banning blacks from entering Little Rock Central High School in 1957 after a Supreme Court desegregation ruling

Charles Joseph Finger (1869-1941), British-born adventure writer; received the 1925 Newbery Medal for *Tales from Silver Lands;* left home at age sixteen and traveled all over the world; in his fifties he bought a farm in Fayetteville, settled down, and began writing, drawing from his own adventures for background material; published some thirty-five books

John Gould Fletcher (1886-1950), born in Little Rock; poet, prose writer, and critic; identified with the Imagist poets; published many volumes of verses, including *The Epic of Arkansas;* received the 1939 Pulitzer Prize in poetry for *Selected Poems*

Alice French (1850-1934), fiction writer; wrote under the pen name Octave Thanet; lived in Arkansas; published many articles and short stories in *Harper's, The Atlantic Monthly,* and other magazines; drew material for many of her stories from her experiences in Lawrence County

James William Fulbright (1905-   ), politician, educator; president of the University of Arkansas (1939-41); U.S. representative from Arkansas (1943-45); U.S. senator (1945-74); chairman of the Senate Foreign Relations Committee (1959-74); outspoken critic of the Vietnam War; sponsored the Fulbright Act of 1946, which established a system of international fellowships; author of several books on American foreign policy

Augustus Hill Garland (1832-1899), politician; grew up in Arkansas; governor of Arkansas (1874-77); U.S. senator (1877-85); U.S. attorney general under President Grover Cleveland (1885-89); first Arkansan appointed to a U.S. cabinet position

Frederick Gerstaecker (1816-1872), German traveler, writer; lived in Arkansas from 1838 to 1841; wrote about Arkansas from the viewpoint of a European; wrote several novels featuring Arkansas frontiersmen, including *The Regulators in Arkansas* and *The River Pirates of the Mississippi*

Donald Harington (1935-   ), born in Little Rock; novelist, art historian; his writings reflect the industriousness and simple charm of Arkansas's people; books include *Architecture of the Ozarks, Some Other Place: The Right Place,* and *Let Us Build Us a City*

Haroldson Fayette (H.L.) Hunt (1889-1974), businessman; one of the wealthiest people in the world; born in Illinois, he made his fortune on the oil discovered in Arkansas in the 1920s; founded Hunt Oil Company (1936); broadcast his conservative views on a weekly radio show called "Life Line"

John Harold Johnson (1918-   ), born in Arkansas City; publisher; founder and president of Johnson Publishing Company, which produces *Ebony* magazine and is the leading black-owned business in the United States

E. Fay Jones (1921-   ), architect; director of the school of architecture at the University of Arkansas; designed the legendary Thorncrown Chapel near Eureka Springs, a rustic but elegant structure of glass set in the wilderness

Bénard de La Harpe (1683-1765), French explorer; in 1722 spotted the rocky promontory on the Arkansas River bank that became known as the Little Rock

Douglas MacArthur (1880-1964), born in Little Rock; military leader; served in France during World War I and rose from the rank of major to brigadier general; commander of Allied forces in the Southwest Pacific during World War II; commanded United Nations forces defending South Korea during the Korean conflict; most famous quote, regarding his intention to defend the Philippines from the Japanese, was "I shall return"

John Little McClellan (1896-1977), born near Sheridan; politician; U.S. representative (1935-39); U.S. senator (1942-77); chairman of the Senate's Permanent Investigations Subcommittee (1955-73), which investigated organized crime and labor unions; chairman of the Senate Appropriations Committee (1973-77); cosponsored the McClellan-Kerr Arkansas River Navigation System project

Wilbur Daigh Mills (1909-   ), born in Kensett; politician; U.S. representative (1939-77); as chairman of the House Ways and Means Committee (1958-75), exerted great influence over tax and other financial legislation

AUGUSTUS GARLAND

H.L. HUNT

JOHN McCLELLAN

WILBUR MILLS

ISAAC PARKER

JOSEPH ROBINSON

WINTHROP ROCKEFELLER

URIAH MILTON ROSE

Sidney Moncrief (1957-   ), born in Little Rock; professional basketball player; during the 1971-72 season, broke Kareem Abdul-Jabbar's record of 504 free throws; named Defensive Player of the Year by the National Basketball Association in 1983 and 1984

Isaac Charles Parker (1838-1896), judge; presided over the federal district court at Fort Smith (1875-96); known as the "Hanging Judge," he had jurisdiction over western Arkansas and all of Indian Territory; sentenced 177 men to the gallows during his years on the bench, causing outlaws to call Fort Smith "hell on the border"

Albert Pike (1809-1891), poet, writer, teacher, lawyer, and soldier; moved from Massachusetts to Arkansas in 1832; served in Arkansas's territorial legislature; fought in the Mexican War (1846-48); led a Confederate brigade of Cherokee Indians in the Civil War Battle of Pea Ridge (1862)

Vance Randolph (1892-1982), Ozark folklorist; lived in Fayetteville and published several collections of Ozark folk tales, legends, superstitions, and other traditional materials

Opie Percival Read (1852-1939), journalist, novelist, and playwright; moved to Arkansas in the 1870s and became city editor of the *Arkansas Gazette*; founded the humorous literary journal *The Arkansaw Traveler* in 1882 and continued publishing it in Chicago in 1887; as a writer, often portrayed hillbillies and southern gentlemen; author of more than fifty books, including *A Kentucky Colonel, A Tennessee Judge,* and *An Arkansas Planter*

Mary Elsie Robertson (1937-   ), born in Charleston; writer; uses local Arkansas country characters, settings, and folk customs in her short stories, novels, and children's books

Joseph Taylor Robinson (1872-1937), born near Lonoke; politician; U.S. representative (1903-13); governor of Arkansas (1913); U.S. senator (1913-37); Senate minority leader (1923); vice-presidential running mate of Democratic presidential candidate Alfred E. Smith (1928); Senate majority leader (1933-37)

Winthrop Rockefeller (1912-1973), politician, cattleman; moved from New York to Arkansas in 1953 and set up Winrock Farms, a ranch known for its hardy Santa Gertrudis cattle; appointed director of the Arkansas Industrial Development Commission (AIDC) in 1955; defeated Governor Orval Faubus in 1966, becoming Arkansas's first Republican governor since Reconstruction (1967-71)

Uriah Milton Rose (1834-1913), distinguished lawyer; settled in Arkansas and helped set high standards for the legal profession there; in 1907 represented America at the International Peace Conference at The Hague in The Netherlands; his statue, representing Arkansas, stands in Statuary Hall in the U.S. Capitol in Washington, D.C.

William Grant Still (1895-1987), grew up in Little Rock; composer; in 1936, became the first black to conduct an American professional symphony orchestra; best-known work is *Afro-American Symphony*

Edward Durell Stone (1902-1978), born in Fayetteville; architect; known for his designs using concrete to screen the sun's rays; among his most famous buildings are the Museum of Modern Art in New York City, the Kennedy Center for the Performing Arts in Washington, D.C., and the Standard Oil Building in Chicago; his buildings in Arkansas include the University of Arkansas's Fine Arts Center and Pine Bluff's Civic Center

EDWARD DURELL STONE

Ruth McEnery Stuart (1849-1917), writer; lived in Washington, Arkansas, from 1879 to 1883; used her Arkansas experiences to create the imaginary town of Simpkinsville; her stories of southern life include *The Unlived Life of Little Mary Ellen* and *Daddy Do-Funny's Wisdom Jingles*

David Thibault (1892-1934), born in Little Rock; writer; his stories appeared in *Collier's* and *Harper's* magazines; after he died of meningitis, his story "A Woman Like Dilsie" appeared in the *O. Henry Memorial Award Prize Stories of 1937*

SAM WALTON

Henri de Tonti (1650-1704), French explorer; accompanied La Salle down the Mississippi River in 1682; in 1686 returned to what is now Arkansas and established Arkansas Post, the first permanent white settlement in the lower Mississippi River Valley

Sam M. Walton (1918-   ), business executive; worked with J.C. Penney and Ben Franklin stores in the 1940s and 1950s; since 1962, has been chairman of his own Wal-Mart Stores, based in Bentonville

William Caesar Warfield (1920-   ), born in West Helena; concert singer, actor, educator; appeared in the movie *Showboat* in 1951; sang the role of Porgy in a government-sponsored European production of George Gershwin's *Porgy and Bess*; has made numerous appearances as a concert soloist and has appeared in many operas

WILLIAM WARFIELD

Charles Morrow Wilson (1905-   ), born in Fayetteville; writer; deals with many subjects, including life in his beloved Ozarks; his books include *Acres of Sky*, *Meriwether Lewis*, and *Backwoods America*

Thyra Samter Winslow (1893-1961), novelist and short-story writer; her works appeared in such magazines as *New Yorker*, *Cosmopolitan*, and *Smart Set*; many of her harsh and realistic stories are based on her experiences in Fort Smith

William Edward Woodruff (1795-1885), journalist; in 1819, at Arkansas Post, founded the *Arkansas Gazette*, the oldest newspaper west of the Mississippi River

THYRA SAMTER WINSLOW

ARCHIBALD YELL

Comer Vann (C. Vann) Woodward (1908-   ), born in Vanndale; historian and educator; Sterling Professor of History at Yale University (1961-77); received the 1982 Pulitzer Prize in history for his editing of *Mary Chestnut's Civil War*

Archibald Yell (1797-1847), judge, politician, military leader; Arkansas territorial judge (1835); first U.S. representative from Arkansas (1837-39, 1845); governor of Arkansas (1840-44); killed during the Mexican War while leading an Arkansas cavalry regiment in the Battle of Buena Vista

GOVERNORS

James S. Conway	1836-1840	Charles H. Brough	1917-1921
Archibald Yell	1840-1844	Thomas C. McRae	1921-1925
Thomas S. Drew	1844-1849	Thomas J. Terral	1925-1927
John Seldon Roane	1849-1852	John E. Martineau	1927-1928
Elias Nelson Conway	1852-1860	Harvey Parnell	1928-1933
Henry M. Rector	1860-1862	Junius M. Futrell	1933-1937
Harris Flanagin		Carl E. Bailey	1937-1941
(Confederate)	1862-1865	Homer M. Adkins	1941-1945
Isaac Murphy (Union)	1864-1868	Benjamin T. Laney	1945-1949
Powell Clayton	1868-1871	Sidney S. McMath	1949-1953
Ozra A. Hadley	1871-1873	Francis Cherry	1953-1955
Elisha Baxter	1873-1874	Orval E. Faubus	1955-1967
Augustus H. Garland	1874-1877	Winthrop Rockefeller	1967-1971
William R. Miller	1877-1881	Dale L. Bumpers	1971-1975
Thomas J. Churchill	1881-1883	Robert C. Riley	1975
James H. Berry	1883-1885	David H. Pryor	1975-1979
Simon P. Hughes	1885-1889	William Clinton	1979-1981
James P. Eagle	1889-1893	Frank D. White	1981-1983
William M. Fishback	1893-1895	William Clinton	1983-
James P. Clarke	1895-1897		
Daniel W. Jones	1897-1901		
Jeff Davis	1901-1907		
John S. Little	1907-1909		
George W. Donaghey	1909-1913		
Joseph T. Robinson	1913		
George W. Hays	1913-1917		

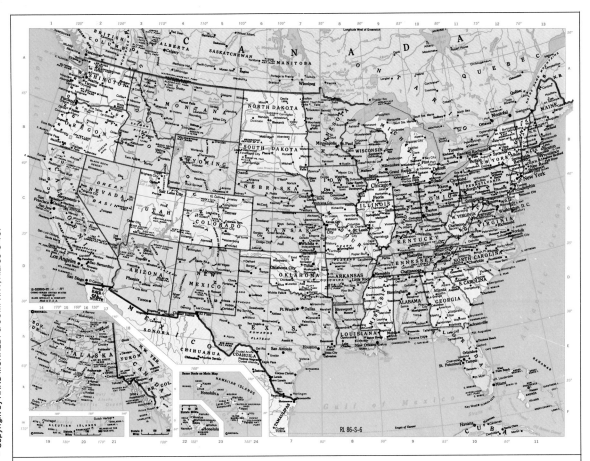

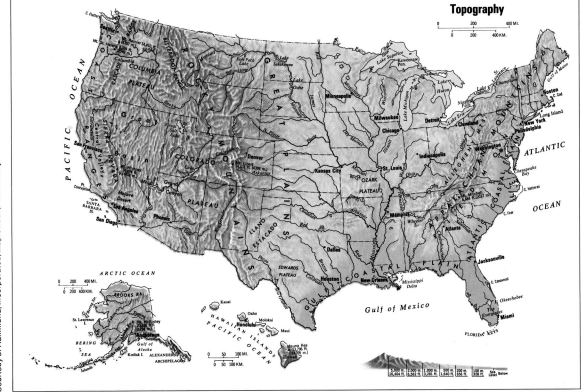

Topography

MAP KEY

Almo B1
Alpena A2
Altheimer C4
Altus B2
Amity C2
Arkadelphia C2
Arkansas City D4
Arkansas River (river) C3
Ash Flat A4
Ashdown D1
Atkins B3
Augusta B4
Bald Knob B4
Baring B1
Bartholomew Bayou (bayou) D4
Batesville B4
Bauxite C3
Bay B5
Bayou des Arc (bayou) B4
Bear Mountain f7
Bearden D3
Beaver Lake (reservoir) A2
Beebe B4
Bella Vista A1
Bellefonte A2
Belleville B2
Benton C3
Bentonville A1
Berryville A2
Big Bayou (bayou) D4
Big Creek (creek) C5
Big Piney Creek (creek) B2
Big Rock Mountain h10
Bigelow B3
Biggers A5
Biscoe C4
Black River (river) A4
Black Rock A4
Blue Mountain B2
Blue Mountain Lake (reservoir) B2
Blytheville B6
Bodcau Creek (creek) D2
Bonanza B1
Bono A5
Booneville B2
Boston Mountains B2
Bradford B4
Bradley D2
Branch B2
Brinkley C4
Brookland A5
Bryant C3
Buckner D2
Buffalo River (river) A3
Bull Shoals A3
Bull Shoals Lake (lake) A3
Cabot B4
Cache River (river) B4
Caddo Mountains C2
Calico Rock A3
Calion D3

Camden D3
Cammack Village C3
Caraway A5
Carlisle C4
Carthage C3
Catherine, Lake (lake) C3
Cave City A4
Cave Springs A1
Centerton A1
Centerville B3
Charleston B1
Cherokee Village A4
Cherry Valley B5
Chicot, Lake (lake) D5
Chidester C2
Clarendon C4
Clarksville B2
Clinton B3
Coal Hill B2
College City A4
Colt B5
Conway B3
Conway Lake (lake) C4
Corning A5
Cossatot River (river) C1
Cotter A3
Cotton Plant B4
Cove C1
Crawfordsville B5
Crooked Creek (creek) A3
Crossett D4
Cowleys Ridge (ridge) B5
Current River (river) A5
Curtis C2
Cushman B4
Danville B2
Dardanelle B2
Dardanelle Lake (reservoir) B2
De Gray Lake (reservoir) C2
De Queen C1
De Vails Bluff C4
De Witt C4
Dermott D4
Delight C2
Des Arc C4
Desha B4
Diaz B4
Dierks C1
Doddridge D1
Donaldson C3
Dorcheat Bayou (bayou) D2
Dover B3
Dumas D4
Dutch Creek (creek) B2
Dyer B2
Dyess B5
Earle B5
El Dorado D3
Elaine C5
Eleven Point River (river) A4
Elm Springs A1
Emerson D2
Emmet D2
England C4
Erling Lake (lake) D2
Eudora D5
Eureka Springs A2
Evening Shade A3
Farmington D3

Fayetteville A1
Flippin A3
Florence A4
Fordyce D3
Foreman D1
Forrest City B5
Fort Smith B1
Fountain Hill D4
Fourche LaFave River (river) C2
Garland D2
Gassville A3
Genevia C3
Gentry A1
Gillett C4
Gilmore B5
Glenwood C2
Gosnell B6
Gould D4
Grady C4
Granite Mountain C3
Grannis C1
Gravette A1
Gravel Forest B2
Greenbrier B3
Greenland A1
Greenwood B1
Greers Ferry Lake (reservoir) B3
Greeson, Lake (lake) C2
Grubbs B4
Gurdon C2
Hackett B1
Hamburg D4
Hamilton, Lake (lake) C2
Hampton D3
Hardy A4
Harrisburg B5
Harrison A2
Hartford B1
Hartman B2
Haskell C3
Hatfield C1
Hatfield B1
Havana B2
Hazen C4
Heber Springs B3
Hector B3
Helena C5
Hensley C3
Hermitage D3
Hickory Ridge B5
Holly Grove C4
Hope D2
Horatio D1
Hoxie A4
Hudgin Creek (creek) A3
Hughes B5
Humnoke C4
Humphrey C4
Huntington B1
Huntsville A2
Huttig D4
Hurricane Creek (creek) B2
Illinois River (river) A1
Imboden A4
Jacksonville C3
Jasper A2
Johnson A1
Joiner B5
Jones Mill C3
Jonesboro A5
Judsonia B4
Junction City D3
Keiser B5
Kensett B4
Kingsland D3
Kings River (river) A2
Kirby C2
Knobel A5
L'Aigle Creek (creek) D2
La Grue Bayou (bayou) C4
Lake City A5
Lake Hamilton C3
Lake Village D5
Lakeview A3
Lamar B2
Lavaca B1
Leachville B5
Lee Creek (creek) B1
Leola C3
Lepanto B5
Leslie A3
Lewisville D2
Lexa C5
Lincoln A1
Little Mazarn Creek (creek) C2
Little Missouri River (river) C2
Little Red River (river) B4
Little River (river) A1

Little River (river) A1
Little Rock A3
Lockesburg D4
London D1
Lonoke B5
Lost Creek (creek) B1
Lowell D4
Luxora C2
Lynn A5
Mabelvale D2
Mabon Bayou (bayou) k10
Magazine B2
Magazine Mountain B2
Magnolia D2
Malvern C3
Mammoth Spring A4
Manila B5
Mansfield B1
Marianna C5
Marion B5
Marked Tree B5
Marmaduke A5
Marshall A3
Marvell C5
Maumelle Lake (lake) C3
Mayflower B3
Maynard A4
McAlmont C3
McCrory B4
McGehee D4
McNeil D2
McRae B4
Mena C1
Menifee B3
Meto Bayou (bayou) C4
Millwood Lake (reservoir) D1
Mineral Springs D1
Mississippi River (river) B6
Monette A5
Monticello D4
Montrose D4
Moro Creek (creek) D3
Morrilton B3
Moss Mountain C3
Mount Ida C2
Mount Pleasant A4
Mountain Home A3
Mountain Pine C2
Mountain View A3
Mountainburg B1
Mulberry B1
Mulberry Mountain B2
Mulberry River (river) B2
Murfreesboro C2
Nashville D1
New Edinburg D3
Newark B4
Newport A4
Nimrod Lake (reservoir) C2
Norfork A3
Norfork Lake (lake) A3
Norman C2
Norphlet D3
North Crossett D4
North Little Rock C3
Norvell B5
Ola B3
Oppelo B3
Osceola B5
Ouachita Lake (lake) C2
Ouachita River (river) C2
Oxford A4
Ozark B2
Ozark Reservoir (reservoir) B2
Palestine B5
Pangburn B4
Paragould A5
Paris B2
Parkdale D4
Parkin B5
Patterson B4
Pea Ridge A1
Peckerwood Lake (lake) C4
Perryville B3
Petit Jean Creek (creek) B2
Petit Jean Mountain B3
Petit Jean Mountain B3
Piggott A5
Pine Bluff C4
Plainview B3
Plum Bayou (bayou) C4
Plumerville B3
Pocahontas A4
Portia A4

Portland D4
Poteau Mountain C1
Poteau River (river) C1
Pottsville B2
Prairie Grove C1
Prescott D2
Quitman B3
Raspberry Peak C1
Rector A5
Red River (river) k10
Redfield D2
Reyno A5
Rison D3
Robinson Mountain B1
Rogers A1
Roland C3
Russellville B2
Salem A4
Saline River (river) C3
Saline River (river) D4
Searcy B4
Seven Davis Lake (lake) D4
Sharp Top Mountain A2
Sheridan C3
Sherman Mountain C3
Sherwood C3
Shirley A3
Siloam Springs A1
Skylight Mountain h10
Smackover D4
Smackover Creek (creek) D3
Sparkman D2
Spring River (river) B4
St. Francis River (river) B3
Stamps D1
Star City D4
Stephens D2
Stevenson Mountain B1
Strawberry River (river) A4
Strong D3
Stuttgart C4
Subiaco B2
Sulphur River (river) D1
Sulphur Springs A1
Summit A3
Swain Mountain A2
Sweet Home C3
Swifton B4
Sylvan Hills C3
Taylor D2
Texarkana D1
Thornton D3
Toilette D2
Tontitown A1
Trap Mountain g7
Traskwood C3
Trumann B5
Tucker C4
Tuckerman B4
Turrell B5
Tyronzo A5
Urbana D3
Van Buren B1
Viola A3
Violia A4
Wabbaseka C4
Waldo D2
Waldron C2
Walnut Ridge A4
Ward B4
Warren D4
Watson D4
Watson Chapel C4
Weiner B5
West Crossett D4
West Fork A1
West Helena C5
West Memphis B5
Western Grove A3
Wheatley C4
White Hall C4
White Oak Lake (lake) D3
White River (river) D4
Wickes C1
Wilmar D4
Wilmot D5
Wilson B5
Wilton f7
Woodson C4
Wooster k10
Wrightsville B3
Wynne B5
Yellville A3

© Copyright by RAND McNALLY & COMPANY, R.L. 88-S-137

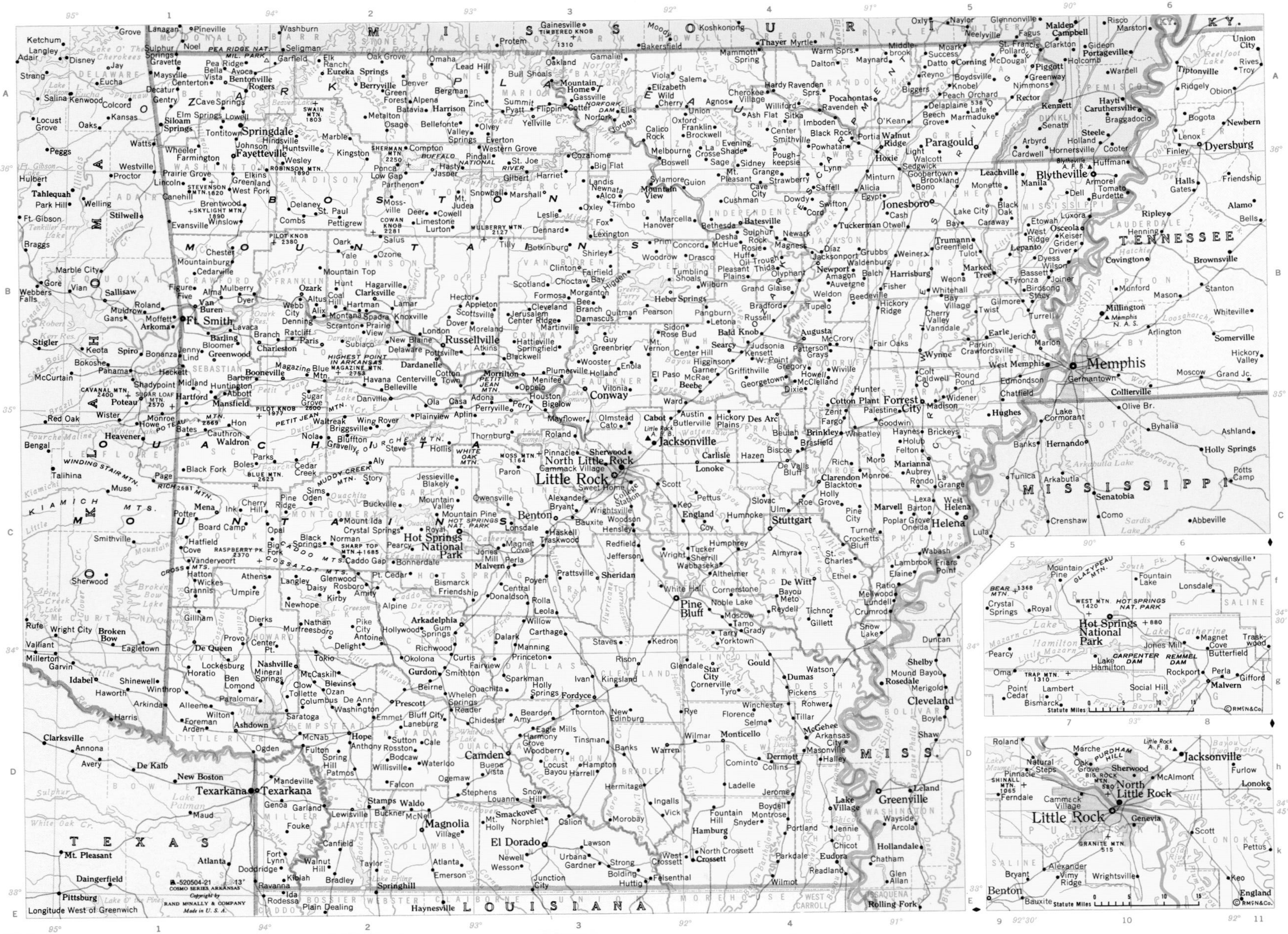

Longitude West of Greenwich

11

Little Rock

Hot Springs National Park

Benton

North Little Rock

KY.

TENNESSEE

MISSISSIPPI

Memphis

MISSOURI

OZARK

OUACHITA

LOUISIANA

TEXAS

Little Rock

Texarkana

El Dorado

Pine Bluff

Hot Springs

Fort Smith

Jonesboro

Paragould

Blytheville

Springdale

Fayetteville

Conway

Dyersburg

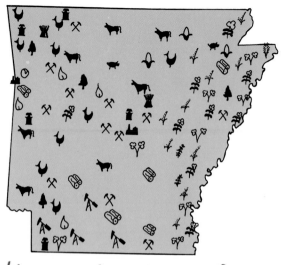

POULTRY
MINING
COTTON
WHEAT
HOGS
CORN

BEEF CATTLE
MANUFACTURING
DAIRY PRODUCTS
NATURAL GAS
VEGETABLES
FRUIT

OATS
OIL
RICE
HAY
FOREST PRODUCTS
SOYBEANS

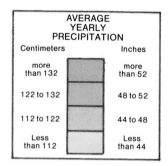

AVERAGE
YEARLY
PRECIPITATION

Centimeters		Inches
more than 132		more than 52
122 to 132		48 to 52
112 to 122		44 to 48
Less than 112		Less than 44

MAJOR HIGHWAYS

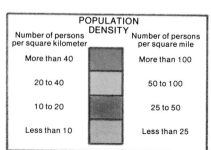

POPULATION
DENSITY

Number of persons per square kilometer		Number of persons per square mile
More than 40		More than 100
20 to 40		50 to 100
10 to 20		25 to 50
Less than 10		Less than 25

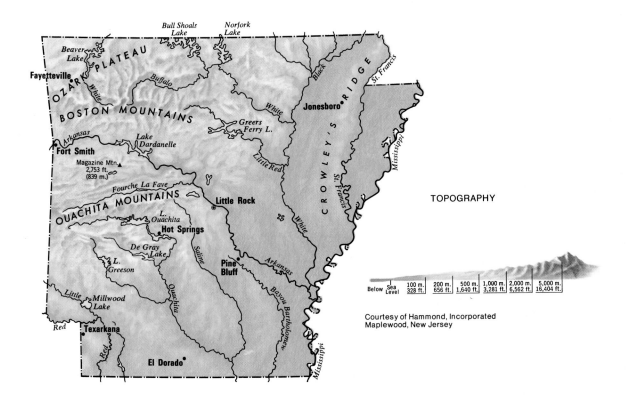

Bull Shoals Lake
Norfork Lake
Beaver Lake
Fayetteville
OZARK PLATEAU
Buffalo
White
BOSTON MOUNTAINS
Black
St. Francis
Jonesboro
Greers Ferry L.
White
CROWLEY'S RIDGE
Lake Dardanelle
Arkansas
Little Red
Fort Smith
Magazine Mtn.
2,753 ft.
(839 m.)
Fourche La Fave
St. Francis
Mississippi
OUACHITA MOUNTAINS
Little Rock
L. Ouachita
Hot Springs
White
De Gray Lake
Saline
L. Greeson
Pine Bluff
Arkansas
Ouachita
Bayou Bartholomew
Little
Millwood Lake
Red
Texarkana
Red
El Dorado
Mississippi

TOPOGRAPHY

| Below Sea Level | 100 m. 328 ft. | 200 m. 656 ft. | 500 m. 1,640 ft. | 1,000 m. 3,281 ft. | 2,000 m. 6,562 ft. | 5,000 m. 16,404 ft. |

Courtesy of Hammond, Incorporated
Maplewood, New Jersey

COUNTIES

Bentonville
BENTON
Eureka Springs
Berryville
CARROLL
BOONE
Harrison
MARION
Yellville
Mountain Home
BAXTER
FULTON
Salem
RANDOLPH
Corning
Piggott
CLAY
Huntsville
MADISON
Jasper
NEWTON
Marshall
SEARCY
IZARD
Melbourne
Ash Flat
SHARP
Pocahontas
LAWRENCE
Walnut Ridge
Paragould
GREENE
Blytheville
Fayetteville
WASHINGTON
STONE
Mountain View
INDEPENDENCE
Batesville
Newport
CRAIGHEAD
Jonesboro
Lake City
MISSISSIPPI
Osceola
CRAWFORD
FRANKLIN
Ozark
Van Buren
JOHNSON
Clarksville
Clinton
VAN BUREN
CLEBURNE
Heber Springs
JACKSON
POINSETT
Harrisburg
Ft Smith
Charleston
Greenwood
SEBASTIAN
LOGAN
Paris
Booneville
POPE
Russellville
Dardanelle
CONWAY
Morrilton
FAULKNER
Conway
Perryville
WHITE
Searcy
Augusta
WOODRUFF
CROSS
Wynne
Marion
CRITTENDEN
Danville
YELL
PERRY
PULASKI
LITTLE ROCK
SALINE
Lonoke
LONOKE
Des Arc
PRAIRIE
DeValls Bluff
MONROE
Clarendon
ST FRANCIS
Forrest City
LEE
Marianna
SCOTT
Mena
POLK
Mount Ida
MONTGOMERY
GARLAND
Hot Springs
Benton
Malvern
HOT SPRING
Sheridan
GRANT
JEFFERSON
Pine Bluff
ARKANSAS
DeWitt
Stuttgart
Helena
PHILLIPS
De Queen
SEVIER
PIKE
Murfreesboro
Arkadelphia
CLARK
DALLAS
Fordyce
Rison
CLEVELAND
Star City
LINCOLN
DESHA
HOWARD
Nashville
LITTLE RIVER
Ashdown
HEMPSTEAD
Hope
Prescott
NEVADA
OUACHITA
Camden
CALHOUN
Hampton
BRADLEY
Warren
Monticello
DREW
Arkansas City
Lake Village
Texarkana
MILLER
Lewisville
LAFAYETTE
Magnolia
COLUMBIA
UNION
El Dorado
Hamburg
ASHLEY
CHICOT

An agricultural pilot in Wilson refuels at the end of a long day.

INDEX

Page numbers that appear in boldface type indicate illustrations.

**Metrocentre Mall in
downtown Little Rock**

Picture Identifications

Front Cover: Sunset Point, Petit Jean Mountain
Back Cover: Skyline of Little Rock
Pages 2-3: Geese on the White River near Lakeview
Page 6: The state capitol in Little Rock
Pages 8-9: Buffalo National River
Pages 18-19: Montage of Arkansas residents
Pages 26-27: La Salle among the Quapaws at the mouth of the Arkansas River
Pages 36-37: *The Turn of the Tune*, an 1870 lithograph by Currier & Ives showing a traveler playing the celebrated tune "The Arkansas Traveler"
Page 50: An 1890 photograph of a railroad station in Little Rock
Pages 60-61: Pulpwood chips being readied for processing at an Arkansas paper mill
Page 74: Montage showing Arkansas's rich folk heritage
Pages 80-81: Canoeing on the Buffalo National River
Pages 90-91: Little Rock at night
Page 108: Montage showing the state flag, the state tree (pine), the state insect (honeybee), the state musical instrument (fiddle), the state gem (diamond), and the state flower (apple blossom)

Picture Acknowledgments

H. Armstrong Roberts: © J. Buehner: Front cover; © H. Abernathy: Back cover
Photo Options: © Steve Price: Pages 2-3, 14 (left), 87 (top right); © Ed Malles: Page 16 (alligator); © Michael Clemmer: Page 74 (bottom left)
Shostal Associates: Pages 63, 66 (right), 108 (honeybee, diamonds); © Tom Coker: Pages 4, 11, 121; © Bill Barley: Pages 60-61; © Ed Cooper: Page 105 (left); © Eric Carle: Pages 108 (pines), 119 (left); © Sal Maimone: Page 108 (apple blossoms)
Root Resources: © Garry D. McMichael: Pages 5, 67 (right), 68 (top right), 69 (left, bottom right), 72, 74 (bottom right), 77 (right), 93 (left), 98 (left), 99, 103, 106 (bottom right), 117; © Bill Barksdale: Pages 13, 69 (top right), 95, 101; © Vera Bradshaw: Pages 76 (right), 112
Gartman Agency: © Mark E. Gibson: Page 6
© **Matt Bradley:** Pages 8-9, 12, 16 (sumac, phlox, cypress), 18, 19, 21, 22 (right), 23, 66 (center), 67 (left), 68 (left, bottom right), 74 (top left, top right, bottom center), 76 (left), 80-81, 87 (top left, bottom left, bottom right), 89, 90-91, 93 (right), 94, 98 (center, right), 100, 113, 115, 119 (right), 120, 138, 141
© **Franke Keating:** Pages 14 (right), 22 (left), 74 (middle right), 77 (left), 106 (top right)
© **Lynn M. Stone:** Pages 16 (deer, snake, opossum), 114
National Gallery of Art: Pages 26-27
Arkansas Department of Parks & Tourism: Pages 29 (large photo), 39, 83, 84, 97, 108 (fiddler), 122
Arkansas Archaeological Survey: Pages 29 (inset), 30 (top left)
Historical Pictures Service Inc., Chicago: Pages 30 (top right), 55, 57 (right), 85 (left), 128 (Cleaver, Faubus), 129 (Garland), 130 (Parker), 131 (Warfield)
Toltec Mounds State Park: Page 30 (bottom)
North Wind Picture Archives: Pages 33 (top left), 46, 124, 130 (Rose)
Library of Congress: Page 33 (top right)
The Granger Collection: Pages 33 (bottom left, bottom center), 36-37, 42, 44
Arkansas History Commission: Pages 33 (bottom right), 48, 50, 53, 57 (left), 127 (Angelou), 132
St. Louis Globe Democrat, **Courtesy of Arkansas History Commission:** Page 35
© **Henry Francis du Pont Winterthur Museum:** Page 40 (left)
National Archives: Page 40 (right)
Minnesota Historical Society: Page 45
University of Arkansas at Little Rock Archives: Pages 54, 131 (Winslow)
Culver Pictures, Inc.: Pages 56, 85 (right), 129 (McClellan)
TSW-Click/Chicago: © Don Smetzer: Pages 59 (left), 66 (left)
Photri: © Les Riess: Pages 59 (right), 105 (right), 106 (top left, bottom left)
© **M.L. Dembinsky, Jr.:** Pages 64, 70
Wide World Photos: Pages 85 (center), 127 (Anthony, Campbell, Caraway), 128 (Dean, Fulbright), 129 (Hunt, Mills), 130 (Robinson, Rockefeller), 131 (Stone, Walton)
Len W. Meents: Maps on pages 93, 97, 99, 103, 105, 136
Courtesy Flag Research Center, Winchester, Massachusetts: Flag on page 108

About the Author

Ann Heinrichs was born and raised in Fort Smith, Arkansas, and spent her childhood roaming the blackberry patches and woods. Now a free-lance writer and editor living in Chicago, Ms. Heinrichs has worked for such educational publishers as Encyclopaedia Britannica, World Book Encyclopedia, and Science Research Associates. As a music critic and feature writer, her articles have appeared in a number of publications. For Childrens Press she has authored *I Can be a Chef, The Hopi,* and several books in the *America the Beautiful* series.